THE FOREIGN INTELLIGENCE SURVEILLANCE ACT

THE FOREIGN INTELLIGENCE SURVEILLANCE ACT

ELIZABETH B. BAZAN

Novinka Books
New York

Library of Congress Cataloging-in-Publication Data

Bazan, Elizabeth B.
The Foreign Intelligence Surveillance Act / Elizabeth B. Bazan
p. cm.
Includes index.
ISBN: 1-59033-495-7.
1. Intelligence service—Law and legislation—United States. 2. National security—Law and legislation—United States. 3. Eavesdropping—United States. 4. Wiretapping—United States. I. Title.

KF4850 .B39 2002
343.73'01—dc21

2002023967

Nova Science Publishers, Inc.
400 Oser Ave, Suite 1600
Hauppauge, New York 11788-3619
Tele. 631-231-7269 Fax 631-231-8175
e-mail: Novascience@earthlink.net
Web Site: http://www.novapublishers.com

Printed in the United States of America

CONTENTS

PREFACE

One of the sharpest debates being played out during America's war on terror pits the government's national security interests against an individual's right to privacy. Recent amendments to the Foreign Intelligence Surveillance Act have given the government expanded powers for electronic investigation under the act. Many have voiced concerns that with such broad rules the personal freedoms enshrined in American tradition are in danger, despite the protestations of federal officials who say they will not abuse their authority. Given the current threats to U.S. security and revelations about intelligence failures leading to September 11, 2001, there is a case to be made that national security trumps individual liberty in certain cases. As questions arise over "battlefield detainees" and the fate of those held for undisclosed violations, the importance of law enforcement regulations takes center stage.

This book provides an overview and analysis of one the United States' most crucial intelligence gathering statutes. In order to fully comprehend the domestic battles being waged over the proper balance between national security and personal liberty, the study presented here is an invaluable resource.

SUMMARY

The Foreign Intelligence Surveillance Act, 50 U.S C. § 1801 *et seq.*, provides a statutory framework for electronic surveillance in the context of foreign intelligence gathering. In so doing, the Congress sought to strike a delicate balance between national security interests and personal privacy rights. Subsequent legislation expanded federal laws dealing with foreign intelligence gathering to address physical searches, pen registers and trap and trace devices, and access to certain business records. P.L. 107-56 made significant changes to some of these provisions. This report will examine the detailed statutory structure provided by the Foreign Intelligence Surveillance Act, as amended (FISA), and related provisions of E.O. 12333. It is current through the changes to FISA in the Uniting and Strengthening America by Providing Appropriate Tools Required to Intercept and Obstruct Terrorism (USA PATRIOT) Act of 2001, P.L. 107-56, which was signed into law by President George W. Bush on October 26, 2001, and the amendments included in the Intelligence Authorization Act for Fiscal Year 2002, P.L. 107-108, which was signed into law by the President on December 28, 2001.

Chapter 1

INTRODUCTION

On October 26, 2001, President George W. Bush signed P.L. 107-56, the Uniting and Strengthening America by Providing Appropriate Tools Required to Intercept and Obstruct Terrorism Act or the USA PATRIOT Act. Among its provisions are a number which impacted or amended the Foreign Intelligence Surveillance Act, 50 U.S.C. § 1801 *et seq*. (FISA). For example, the new law expanded the number of United States district court judges on the Foreign Intelligence Surveillance Court and provided for roving or multipoint electronic surveillance authority under FISA. It also amended FISA provisions with respect to pen registers and trap and trace devices and access to business records. In addition, FISA, as amended, substantially expanded the reach of the business records provisions. The amended language changed the certification demanded of a federal officer applying for a FISA order for electronic surveillance from requiring a certification that *the* purpose of the surveillance is to obtain foreign intelligence information to requiring certification that *a significant purpose* of the surveillance is to obtain foreign intelligence information. FISA, as amended, also affords persons aggrieved by inappropriate use or disclosure of information gathered in or derived from a FISA surveillance, physical search or use of a pen register or trap and trace device a private right of action. Of the amendments made by the USA PATRIOT Act, all but the section which increased the number of judges on the Foreign Intelligence Surveillance Court will sunset on December 31, 2005.

This report will provide background on the Foreign Intelligence Surveillance Act, and discuss its statutory framework, as modified by P.L. 107-56. Where applicable, this report will also note the amendments to FISA reflected in P.L. 107-108 (H.R. 2883), the Intelligence Authorization Act for

Fiscal Year 2002, which was signed into law by the President on December 28, 2001.

BACKGROUND

Investigations for the purpose of gathering foreign intelligence give rise to a tension between the Government's legitimate national security interests and the protection of privacy interests.[1] The stage was set for legislation to address these completing concerns in part by Supreme Court decisions on related issues. In *Katz v. United States*, 389 U.S. 347 (1967), the Court held that the protections of the Fourth Amendment extended to circumstances involving electronic surveillance of oral communications without physical intrusion.[2] The *Katz* Court stated, however, that its holding did not extend to cases involving national security.[3] In *United States v. United States District Court*, 407 U.S. 297 (1972) (the *Keith* case), the Court regarded *Katz* as "implicitly recogniz[ing] that the broad and unsuspected governmental incursions into conversational privacy which electronic surveillance entails necessitate the application of Fourth Amendment safeguards."[4] Mr. Justice Powell, writing for the *Keith* Court, framed the matter before the Court as follows:

> The issue before us is an important one for the people of our country and their Government. It involves the delicate question of the President's power, acting through the Attorney General, to authorize electronic surveillance in internal security matter without prior judicial approval. Successive Presidents for more than one-quarter of a century have authorized such surveillance in varying degrees, without guidance from the Congress or a definitive decision of this Court. This case brings the issue here for the first time. Its resolution is a matter of national concern, requiring sensitivity both to the Government's right to protect itself from unlawful subversion and attack and to the citizen's right to be secure in his privacy against unreasonable Government intrusion.[5]

---

[1] The Fourth Amendment to the United States Constitution states:

> The right of the people to be secure in their persons, houses, papers, and effects, against unreasonable searches and seizures, shall not be violated, and no Warrants shall issue, but upon probably cause, supported by Oath or affirmation, and particularly describing the place to be searched, and the persons or things to be seized.

[2] *Katz v. United States*, 389 U.S. 347,353 (1967).

[3] *Id.*, at 359, n. 23.

[4] *United States v. United States District Court*, 407 U.S. 297, 313-14 (1972).

[5] 407 U.S. at 299.

The Court held that, in the case of intelligence gathering involving domestic security surveillance, prior judicial approval was required to satisfy the Fourth Amendment.[6] Justice Powell emphasized that the case before it "require[d] no judgment on the scope of the president's surveillance power with respect to the activities of foreign powers, within or without the country."[7] The Court expressed no opinion as to "the issues which may be involved with respect to activities of foreign powers or their agents."[8] However, the guidance which the Court provided in *Keith* with respect to national security surveillance in a domestic context to some degree presaged the approach Congress was to take in foreign intelligence surveillance. The *Keith* Court observed in part:

> ... We recognize that domestic surveillance may involve different policy and practical considerations from the surveillance of "ordinary crime." The gathering of security intelligence is often long range and involves the interrelation of various sources and types of information. The exact targets of such surveillance may be more difficult to identify than in surveillance operations against many types of crime specified in Title III [of the Omnibus Crime Control and Safe Streets Act, 18 U.S.C. § 2510 *et seq.*]. Often, too, the emphasis of domestic intelligence gathering is on the prevention of unlawful activity or the enhancement of the Government's preparedness for some possible future crisis or emergency. Thus, the focus of domestic surveillance may be less precise than that directed against more conventional types of crime. Given these potential distinctions between Title III criminal surveillances and those involving domestic security, Congress may wish to consider protective standards for the latter which differ from those already prescribed for specified crimes in Title III. Different standards may be compatible with the Fourth Amendment if they are reasonable both in relation to the legitimate need of Government for intelligence information and the protected rights of our citizens. For the warrant application may vary according to the governmental interest to be enforced and the nature of citizen rights deserving protection.... It may be that Congress, for example, would judge that the application and affidavit

---

[6] *Id.*, at 391-321. Justice Powell also observed that,

> National security cases ... often reflect a convergence of First and Fourth Amendment values not present in cases of "ordinary" crime. Though the investigative duty of the executive may be stronger in such cases, so also is there greater jeopardy to constitutionally protected speech. "Historically the struggle for freedom of speech and press in England was bound up with the issue of the scope of the search and seizure power," *Marcus v. Search Warrant*, 367 U.S. 717,724 (1961). ... Fourth Amendment protections become the more necessary when the targets of official surveillance may be those suspected of unorthodoxy in their political beliefs. The danger to political dissent is acute where the Government attempts to act under so vague a concept as the power to protect "domestic security."

[7] *Id.*, at 308.

[8] *Id.*, at 321-22.

> showing probable cause need not follow the exact requirements of § 2518 but should allege other circumstances more appropriate to domestic security cases; that the request for prior court authorization could, in sensitive cases, be made to any member of a specially designated court…; and that the time and reporting requirements need not be so strict as those in § 2518. The above paragraph does not, of course, attempt to guide the congressional judgment but rather to delineate the present scope of our own opinion. We do not attempt to detail the precise standards for domestic security warrants any more than our decision in *Katz* sought to set the refined requirements for the specified criminal surveillances which now constitute Title III. We do hold, however, that prior judicial approval is required for the type of domestic surveillance involved in this cases and that such approval may be made in accordance with such reasonable standards as the Congress may prescribe.[9]

Court of appeals decisions following *Keith* met more squarely the issue of warrantless electronic surveillance in the context of foreign intelligence gathering. In *United States v. Brown*, 484 F.2d 418 (5th Cir. 1973), *cert. denied,* 415 U.S. 960 (1974), The Fifth Circuit upheld the legality of a warrantless wiretap authorized by the Attorney General for foreign intelligence purposes where the conversation of Brown, an American citizen, was incidentally overheard. The Third Circuit in *United States v. Butenko*, 494 F.23 593 (rd Cir. 1974), *cert. denied sub nom, Ivanov v. United States*, 419 U.S. 881 (1974), concluded that warrantless electronic surveillance was lawful, violating neither Section 605 of the Communications Act nor the Fourth Amendment, if its primary purpose was to gather foreign intelligence information. In its plurality decision in *Zweibon v. Mitchell*, 516 F.2d 594, 613-14 (D.C. Cir. 1975), *cert. denied*, 425 U.S. 944 (1976), the District of Columbia Circuit took a somewhat different view in a case involving a warrantless wiretap of a domestic organization that was not an agent of a foreign power or working in collaboration with a foreign power. Finding that a warrant was required in such circumstances, the plurality also noted that "an analysis of the policies implicated by foreign security surveillance indicates that, absent exigent circumstances, all warrantless electronic surveillance is unreasonable and therefore unconstitutional."

With the passage of the Foreign Intelligence Surveillance Act (FISA), P.L. 95-511, Title I, Oct. 25, 1978, 92 Stat. 1796, codified as amendment at 50 U.S.C. § 1801 *et seq*., Congress sought to strike a delicate balance between these interests when the gathering of foreign intelligence involved

[9] 407 U.S. at 323-24.

the use of electronic surveillance.[10] Collection of foreign intelligence information through electronic surveillance is now governed by FISA and E.O. 12333.[11] This report will examine the provisions of FISA which deal with electronic surveillance, in the foreign intelligence context, as well as those applicable to physical searches, the use of pen registers and trap and trace devices under FISA, and access to business records and other tangible things for foreign intelligence purposes. As the provisions of E.O. 12333 to some extent set the broader context within which FISA operates, we will briefly examine its pertinent provisions first.

---

[10] For an examination of the legislative history of P.L. 95-511, see S. Rept. 95-604, Senate Committee on the Judiciary, parts I and II (Nov. 15, 22, 1977); S. Rept. 95-701, Senate Select Committee on Intelligence (March 14, 1978); H. Rept. 95-1283, House Permanent Select Committee on Intelligence (June 8, 1978); H. Conf. Rept. 95-1720 (Oct. 5, 1978); Senate Reports and House Conference Report are reprinted in 1978 *U.S. Code Cong. & Admin. News* 3904.

[11] Physical searches for foreign intelligence information are governed by 50 U.S.C. § 1821 *et seq*., while the use of pen registers and trap and trace devices in connection with foreign intelligence investigations is addressed in 50 U.S.C. § 1841 *et seq*. Access to certain business records for foreign intelligence or international terrorism investigative purposes is covered by 50 U.S.C. § 1861 *et seq*.

Chapter 2

EXECUTIVE ORDER 12333

Under Part 2.3 of E.O. 12333, the agencies within the Intelligence Community are to "collect, retain or disseminate information concerning United States persons only in accordance with procedures established by the head of the agency concerned and approved by the Attorney General, consistent with the authorities provided by Part 1 of this Order…." Among the types of information that can be collected, retained or disseminated under this section are:

(a) Information that is publicly available or collected with the consent of the person concerned;
(b) Information constituting foreign intelligence or counterintelligence, including such information concerning corporations or other commercial organizations. Collection within the United States of foreign intelligence not otherwise obtainable shall be undertaken by the FBI or, when significant foreign intelligence is sought, by other authorized agencies of the Intelligence Community, provided that no foreign intelligence collection by such agencies may be undertaken for the purpose of acquiring information concerning the domestic activities of United States persons;
(c) Information obtained in the course of a lawful foreign intelligence, counterintelligence, international narcotics or international terrorism investigation;
(d) Information needed to protect the safety of any persons or organizations, including those who are targets, victims or hostages of international terrorist organizations;
(e) Information needed to protect foreign intelligence or counter-intelligence sources or methods from unauthorized disclosure. Collection within the United States shall be undertaken by the FBI except that other agencies of the Intelligence Community may also collect such information concerning present or former employees,

present or former intelligence agency contractors or their present or former employees, or applicants for any such employment of contracting;

(f)Info rmation concerning persons who are reasonably believed to be potential sources or contacts for the purpose of determining their suitability or credibility;

(g) Information arising out of a lawful personnel, physical or communications security investigation;

...

(h) Incidentally obtained information that may indicate involvement in activities that may violate federal, state, local or foreign laws; and

(i) Information necessary for administrative purposes.

In addition, agencies within the Intelligence Community may disseminate information, other than information derived from signals intelligence, to each appropriate agency within the Intelligence Community for purposes of allowing the recipient agency to determine whether the information is relevant to its responsibilities and can be retained by it.

In discussing collections techniques, Part 2.4 of E.O. 12333 indicates that agencies within the Intelligence Community are to use

> the least intrusive collection techniques feasible within the United States or directed against United States persons abroad. Agencies are not authorized to use such techniques as electronic surveillance, unconsented physical search, mail surveillance, physical surveillance, or monitoring devices unless they are in accordance with procedures established by the head of the agency concerned and approved by the Attorney General. Such procedures shall protect constitutional and other legal rights and limit use of such information to lawful governmental purposes....

Part 2.5 of the Executive Order 12333 states that:

> The Attorney General hereby is delegated the power to approve the use for intelligence purposes, within the United States or against a United States person abroad, of any technique for which a warrant would be required if undertaken for law enforcement purposes, provided that such techniques shall not be undertaken unless the Attorney General has determined in each case that there is probably cause to believe that the technique is directed against a foreign power or an agent of a foreign power. Electronic surveillance, as defined in the Foreign Intelligence Surveillance Act of 1978 [section 1801 et seq. of this title], shall be conducted in accordance with that Act, as well as this Order.

Chapter 3

THE FOREIGN INTELLIGENCE SURVEILLANCE ACT

THE STATUTORY FRAMEWORK

Electronic Surveillance under FISA

The Foreign Intelligence Surveillance Act (FISA), P.L. 95-511, Title I, Oct. 25, 1978, 92 Stat. 1796, codified at 50 U.S.C. § 1801 *et seq*., as amended, provides a framework for the use of electronic surveillance,[1]

---

[1] 50 U.S.C. § 1801(f)(2) defines "electronic surveillance" to mean:

(1) the acquisition by an electronic, mechanical, or other surveillance device of the contents of any wire or radio communication sent by or intended to be received by a particular, known United States person who is in the United States, if the contents are acquired by intentionally targeting that United States person, under circumstances in which a person has a reasonable expectation of privacy and a warrant would be required for law enforcement purposes;

(2) the acquisition by an electronic, mechanical, or other surveillance device of the contents of any wire communication to or from a person in the United States, without the consent of any person thereto, if such acquisition occurs in the United States, *but does not include the acquisition of those communications of computer trespassers that would be permissible under section 2511(2)(i) of Title 18*;

(3) the intentional acquisition by an electronic, mechanical, or other surveillance device of the contents of any radio communication, under circumstances in which a person has a reasonable expectation of privacy and a warrant would be required for law enforcement purposes, and if both the sender and all intended recipients are located within the United States; or

(4) the installation or use of an electronic, mechanical, or other surveillance device in the United States for monitoring to acquire information, other than from a wire or radio communication, under circumstances in which a person has a reasonable expectation of privacy and a warrant would be required for law enforcement purposes.

The italicized portion of Subsection 1801(f)(2) was added by Sec. 1003 of P.L. 107-56.

physical searches, pen registers and trap and trace devices to acquire foreign intelligence information.[2] This measure seeks to strike a balance between national security needs in the context of foreign intelligence gathering and privacy rights.

Under 50 U.S.C. § 1802, the President, through the Attorney General, may authorize electronic surveillance to acquire foreign intelligence information for up to one year without a court order if two criteria are satisfied. First, to utilize this authority, the Attorney General must certify in writing under oath that:

> (A) the electronic surveillance is solely directed at –
>
> (i) the acquisition of the contents of communications transmitted by means of communications used exclusively between or among

---

[2] "Foreign intelligence information" is defined in 50 U.S.C. § 1801(e) to mean:

> (1) information that relates to, and if concerning a United States person is necessary to, the ability of the United States to protect against –
>
> (A) actual or potential attack of other grave hostile acts of a foreign power or an agent of a foreign power;
>
> (B) sabotage or international terrorism by a foreign power or an agent of a foreign power;
>
> (C) clandestine intelligence activities by an intelligence service or network of a foreign power or by an agent of a foreign power; or
>
> (2) information with respect to a foreign power or foreign territory that relates to, and if concerning a United States person is necessary to –
>
> (A) the national defense or the security of the Unites States; or
>
> (B) the conduct of the foreign affairs of the United States.

"International terrorism" is defined in 50 U.S.C. § 1801(c) to mean activities that:

> (1) involve violent acts or acts dangerous to human life that are a violation of the criminal laws of the United States or of any State, or that would be a criminal violation if committed within the jurisdiction of the United States or any State;
>
> (2) appear to be intended –
>
> (A) to intimidate or coerce a civilian population;
>
> (B) to influence the policy of a government by intimidation or coercion; or
>
> (C) to affect the conduct of a government by assassination or kidnapping; and
>
> (3) occur totally outside the United States, or transcend national boundaries in terms of the means by which they are accomplished, the persons they appear intended to coerce or intimidate, or the locale in which their perpetrators operate or seek asylum.

"Sabotage is defined in 50 U.S.C. § 1801(d) to mean "activities that involve a violation of chapter 105 of Title 18, or that would involve such a violation if committed against the United States."

foreign powers, as defined in section 1801(a)(1), (2), or (3) of this title; or

(ii) the acquisition of technical intelligence, other than the spoken communications of individuals, from property or premises under the open and exclusive control of a foreign power, as defined in section 1801(a)(1), (2) or (3) of this title;

(B) there is no substantial likelihood that the surveillance will acquire the contents of any communication to which a United States person is a party; and

(C) the proposed minimization procedures under section 1801(h) of this title;[3]

---

[3] Minimization procedures with respect to electronic surveillance are defined in 50 U.S.C. § 1801(h) to mean:

(1) specific procedures, which shall be adopted by the Attorney General, that are reasonably designed in light of the purpose and technique of the particular surveillance, to minimize the acquisition and retention, and prohibit the dissemination, of nonpublicly available information concerning unconsenting United States persons consistent with the need of the United States to obtain, produce, and disseminate foreign intelligence information;

(2) procedures that require that nonpublicly available information, which is not foreign intelligence information, as defined in subsection (e)(1) of this section, shall not be disseminated in a manner that identifies any United States person, without such person's consent, unless such person's identity is necessary to understand foreign intelligence information or assess its importance;

(3) notwithstanding paragraphs (1) and (2), procedures that allow for the retention and dissemination of information that is evidence of a crime which has been, is being, or is about to be committed and that is to be retained or disseminated for law enforcement purposes; and

(4) notwithstanding paragraphs (1), (2), and (3), with respect to any electronic surveillance approved pursuant to section 1802(a) of this title, procedures that require that no contents of any communication to which a United States person is a party shall be disclosed, disseminated, or used for any purpose or retained for longer than 72 hours unless a court order under section 1805 of this title is obtained or unless the Attorney General determines that the information indicates a threat of death or serious bodily harm to any person.

Sec. 314(a)(1) of H. Rept. 107-328, the conference report on the Intelligence Authorization Act for Fiscal Year 2002 to accompany H.R. 2883, amended 50 U.S.C. § 1801(h)(4) to change to 72 hours what was previously a 24 hour period beyond which the contents of any communication to which a U.S. person is a party may not be retained absent a court order under 50 U.S.C. § 1805 or a finding by the Attorney General that the information indicates a threat of death or serious bodily injury. The conference version of H.R. 2883 received the approbation of both houses of Congress, and was forwarded to the President on December 18, 2001, for his signature. It became P.L. 107-108.

"United States person" is defined in 50 U.S.C. § 1801(i) to mean

a citizen of the United States, an alien lawfully admitted for permanent residence (as defined in section 1101(a)(20) of Title 8), an unincorporated association a substantial number of members of which are citizens of the United States or aliens lawfully admitted for permanent residence, or a corporation which is incorporated in the United States, but does not include a corporation or an association which is a foreign power, as defined in subsection (a)(1), (2), or (3) of this section.

"Foreign power" is defined in 50 U.S.C. § 1801(a) to mean:

(1) a foreign government or any component thereof, whether or not recognized by the United States;
(2) a faction of a foreign nation or nations, not substantially composed of United States persons:
(3) an entity that is openly acknowledged by a foreign government or governments to be directed and controlled by such foreign government or governments;
(4) a group engaged in international terrorism or activities in preparation therefor;
(5) a foreign-based political organization, not substantially composed of United States persons; or
(6) an entity that is directed and controlled by a foreign government of governments

"Agent of a foreign power" is defined in 50 U.S.C. § 1801(b) to mean:

(1) any person other than a United States person, who—
  (A) acts in the United States as an officer or employee of a foreign power, or as a member of a foreign power as defined in subsection (a)(4) of this section;
  (B) acts for or on behalf of a foreign power which engages in clandestine intelligence activities in the United States contrary to the interests of the United States, when the circumstances of such person's presence in the United States indicate that such person may engage in such activities in the United States, or when such person knowingly aids or abets any person in the conduct of such activities or knowingly conspires with any person to engage in such activities, or;
(2) any person who—
  (A) knowingly engages in clandestine intelligence gathering activities for or on behalf of a foreign power, which activities involve or may involve a violation of the criminal statutes of the United States;
  (B) pursuant to the direction of an intelligence service or network of a foreign power, knowingly engages in any other clandestine intelligence activities for or on behalf of such foreign power, which activities involve or are about to involve a violation of the criminal statutes of the Unites States;
  (C) knowingly engages in sabotage or international terrorism, or activities that are in preparation therefor, or on behalf of a foreign power; or
  (D) knowingly enters the United States under a false or fraudulent identity for or on behalf of a foreign power or, while in the United States, knowingly assumes a false or fraudulent identity for or on behalf of a foreign power, or

Second, in order for the President, through the Attorney General, to use this authority

> … the Attorney General [must report] such minimization procedures and any changes thereto to the House Permanent Select Committee on Intelligence and the Senate Select Committee on Intelligence at least thirty days prior to their effective date, unless the Attorney General determines immediate action is required and notifies the committees immediately of such minimization and the reason for their becoming effective immediately.

Such electronic surveillance must be conducted only in accordance with the Attorney General's certification and minimization procedures adopted by him. A copy of his certification must be transmitted by the Attorney General to the court established under 50 U.S.C. § 1803(a) (hereinafter the FISC).[4] This certification remains under seal unless an application for a court order for surveillance authority is made under 50 U.S.C. §§ 1801(h)(4) and 1804,[5] or the certification is necessary to determine the legality of the surveillance under 50 U.S.C. § 1806(f).[6] 50 U.S.C. § 1802(a)(2) and (a)(3).

In connection with electronic surveillance so authorized, the Attorney General may direct a specified communications common carrier to furnish all information, facilities, or technical assistance needed for the electronic

---

> (E) knowingly aids or abets any person in the conduct of activities described in subparagraph (A), (B), or (C) or knowingly conspires with any person to engage in activities described in subparagraph (A), (B), or (C).

[4] Under 50 U.S.C. § 1803(a), as amended by Section 208 of P.L. 107-56, the Chief Justice of the United States must publicly designate eleven U.S. district court judges from seven of the United States judicial circuits, of whom no fewer than three must reside within 20 miles of the District of Columbia. These eleven judges constitute the court which has jurisdiction over applications for and orders approving electronic surveillance anywhere within the United States under FISA. If an application for electronic surveillance under this Act is denied by one judge of this court, it may not then be considered by another judge on court. If a judge denies such an application, he or she must immediately provide a written statement for the record of the reason(s) for this decision. If the United States so moves, this record must then be transmitted under seal to a court of review established under 50 U.S.C. § 1803(b). The Chief Justice also publicly designates the three U.S. district court or U.S. court of appeals judges who together make up the court of review having jurisdiction to review any denial of an order under FISA. If that court determines that an application was properly denied, again a written record of the reason(s) for the court of review's decision must be provided for the record, and the United States may petition for a writ of certiorari to the United States Supreme Court. All proceedings under this Act must be conducted expeditiously, and the record of all proceedings including applications and orders granted, must be maintained under security measures established by the Chief Justice in consultation with the Attorney General and the Director of Central Intelligence. 50 U.S.C. § 1803(c).

[5] 50 U.S.C. § 1804 is discussed at pages 10-12 of this report, *infra*.

[6] 50 U.S.C. § 1806 is discussed at pages 18-22 of this report, *infra*.

surveillance to be accomplished in a way that would protect its secrecy and minimize interference with the services provided by the carrier to its customers. 50 U.S.C. § 1802(a)(4)(A). In addition, the Attorney General may direct the specified communications common carrier to maintain any records, under security procedures approved by the Attorney General and the Director of Central Intelligence, concerning the surveillance or the assistance provided which the carrier wishes to retain. 50 U.S.C. § 1802(a)(4)(B). Compensation at the prevailing rate must be made to the carrier by the Government for providing such aid.

If the President, by written authorization, empowers the Attorney General to approve applications to the FISC, an application for a court order may be made pursuant to 50 U.S.C. § 1802(b). A judge receiving such an application may grant an order under 50 U.S.C. § 1805 approving electronic surveillance of a foreign power or an agent of a foreign power to obtain foreign intelligence information. There is an exception to this, however. Under 50 U.S.C. § 1802(b), a court does not have jurisdiction to grant an order approving electronic surveillance directed solely as described in 50 U.S.C. § 1802(a)(1)(A) (that is, at acquisition of the contents of communications transmitted by means of communications used exclusively between or among foreign powers, or acquisition of technical intelligence, other than the spoken communications of individuals, from property or premises under the open and exclusive control of a foreign power), unless the surveillance may involve the acquisition of communications of a United States person. 50 U.S.C. § 1802(b).

An application for a court order authorizing electronic surveillance for foreign intelligence purposes may be sought under 50 U.S.C. § 1804. An application for such a court order must be made by a federal officer in writing on oath or affirmation to an FISC judge. The application must be approved by the Attorney General based upon his finding that the criteria and requirements set forth in 50 U.S.C. § 1801 *et seq.*, have been met. Section 1804(a) sets out what must be included in the application:

(1) the identity of the Federal officer making the application;
(2) the authority conferred on the Attorney General by the President of the United States and the approval of the Attorney General to make the application;
(3) the identity, if known, or a description of the target of the electronic surveillance;
(4) a statement of the facts and circumstances relied upon by the applicant to justify his belief that –
    (A) the target of the electronic surveillance is a foreign power or an agent of a foreign power; and

   (B) each of the facilities or places at which the electronic surveillance is directed is being used, or is about to be used, by a foreign power or an agent of a foreign power;

(5) a statement of the proposed minimization procedures;

(6) a detailed description of the nature of the information sought and the type of communications or activities to be subjected to the surveillance;

(7) a certification or certifications by the Assistant to the President for National Security Affairs or an executive branch official or officials designated by the President from among those executive officers employed in the area of national security or defense and appointed by the President with the advice and consent of the Senate[7]

   (A) that the certifying official deems the information sought to be foreign intelligence information;

   (B) that *a significant*[8] purpose of the surveillance is to obtain foreign intelligence information;

---

[7] Under Section 1-103 of Executive Order 12139, the Secretary of State, the Secretary of Defense, the Director of Central Intelligence, the Director of the FBI, the Deputy Secretary of State, the Deputy Secretary of Defense, and the Deputy Director of Central Intelligence were designated to make such certifications in support of applications to engage in electronic surveillance for foreign intelligence purposes. Neither these officials nor anyone acting in those capacities may make such certifications unless they are appointed by the President with the advice and consent of the Senate.

[8] Section 218 of P.L. 107-56 amended the requisite certifications to be made by the Assistant to the President for National Security Affairs, or other designated official (see footnote 18). Heretofore, the certifying official had to certify, among other things, that *the* purpose of the electronic surveillance under FISA was to obtain foreign intelligence information. Under the new language, the certifying official must certify that *a significant* purpose of such electronic surveillance is to obtain foreign intelligence information. This change may have the effect of somewhat blurring the line between electronic surveillance for foreign intelligence purposes and that engaged in for criminal law enforcement purposes.

Past cases considering the constitutional sufficiency of FISA in the context of electronic surveillance have rejected Fourth Amendment challenges and due process challenges under the Fifth Amendment to the use of information gleaned from a FISA electronic surveillance in a subsequent criminal prosecution, because the purpose of the FISA electronic surveillance, both initially and throughout the surveillance, was to secure foreign intelligence information and not primarily oriented towards criminal investigation or prosecution, *United States v. Megahey*, 553 F. Supp. 1180, 1185-1193 (D.N.Y.), *aff'd* 729 F2d 1444 (2d Cir. 1982); *United States v. Ott* 927 F.2d 473, 475 (9th Cir. 1987); *United States v. Badia*, 827 F.23 1458, 1464 (11th Cir. 1987). *See also, United States v. Johnson*, 952 F.2d 565, 572 (1st Cir. 1991), *rehearing and cert. denied*, 506 U.S. 816 (1991) (holding that, although evidence obtained in FISA electronic surveillance may later be used in a criminal prosecution, criminal investigation may not be the primary purpose of the surveillance, and FISA may not be used as an end-run around the 4th Amendment); *United States v. Pelton*, 835 F.2d 1067, 1074-76 (4th Cir. 1987), *cert. denied*, 486 U.S. 1010 (1987) (holding that electronic surveillance under FISA passes constitutional muster where primary purpose of surveillance, initially and throughout surveillance, was gathering of foreign intelligence information; also held that an otherwise valid FISA surveillance was not invalidated because later use of the fruits of the surveillance in criminal prosecution could be anticipated. In addition, the court rejected Pelton's challenge to FISA on the ground that allowing any electronic surveillance on less than the traditional probable cause standard – i.e., probably cause to believe the suspect has

(C) that such information cannot reasonably be obtained by normal investigative techniques;
(D) that designates the type of foreign intelligence information being sought according to the categories described in 1801(e) of this title; and
(E) including a statement of the basis for the certification that –
  (i) the information sought is the type of foreign intelligence information designated; and
  (ii) such information cannot reasonably be obtained by normal investigative techniques.

(8) a statement of the means by which the surveillance will be effected and a statement whether physical entry is required to effect the surveillance;
(9) a statement of the facts concerning all previous applications that have been made to any judge under this subchapter involving any of the persons, facilities, or places specified in the application, and the action taken on each previous application;
(10) a statement of the period of time for which the electronic surveillance is required to be maintained, and if the nature of the intelligence gathering is such that the approval of the use of electronic surveillance under this subchapter should not automatically terminate when the described type of information has first been obtained, a description of facts supporting the belief that additional information of the same type will be obtained thereafter; and
(11) whenever more than one electronic, mechanical or other surveillance device is to be used with respect to a particular proposed electronic surveillance, the coverage of the devices involved and what minimization procedures apply to information acquired by each device.

The application for a court order need not contain the information required in Subsections 1804(6), (7)(E), (8), and (11) above if the target of the electronic surveillance is a foreign power and each of the facilities or places at which surveillance is directed is owned, leased, or exclusively used by that foreign power. However, in those circumstances, the application

---

committed, is committing, or is about to commit a crime for which electronic surveillance is permitted, and that the interception will obtain communications concerning that offense – for issuance of a search warrant was violative of the 4th Amendment, finding FISA's provisions to be reasonable both in relation to the legitimate needs of Government for foreign intelligence information and the protected rights of U.S. citizens); *United States v. Rahman*, 861 F. Supp. 247, 251 (S.D. N.Y. 1994). *Cf.*, *United States v. Bin Laden*, 2001 U.S. Dist. LEXIS 15484 (S.D. N.Y., October 2, 2001); *United States v. Bin Laden*, 126 F. Supp. 264, 277-78 (S.D. N.Y. 2000) (adopting foreign intelligence exception to the warrant requirement for searches targeting foreign powers or agents of foreign powers abroad; noting that this "exception to the warrant requirement applies until and unless the primary purpose of the searches stops being foreign intelligence collection.... If foreign intelligence collection is merely *a* purpose and not the *primary* purpose of a search, the exception does not apply.")

must indicate whether physical entry is needed to effect the surveillance, and must also contain such information about the surveillance techniques and communications or other information regarding United States persons likely to be obtained as may be necessary to assess the proposed minimization procedures. 50 U.S.C. § 1804(b).

Where an application for electronic surveillance under 50 U.S.C. § 1804(a) involves a target described in 50 U.S.C. § 1801(b)(2),[9] the Attorney General must personally review the application if requested to do so, in writing, by the Director of the Federal Bureau of Investigation, the Secretary of Defense, the Secretary of State, or the Director of Central Intelligence.[10] The authority to make such a request may not be delegated unless the official involved is disabled or otherwise unavailable.[11] Each such official must make appropriate arrangements, in advance, to ensure that such a delegation of authority is clearly established in case of disability or other unavailability.[12] If the Attorney General determines that an application should not be approved, he must give the official requesting the Attorney General's personal review of the application written notice of the determination. Except in cases where the Attorney General is disabled or otherwise unavailable, the responsibility for such a determination may not be delegated. The Attorney General must make advance plans to ensure that the delegation of such responsibility where the Attorney General is disabled or otherwise unavailable is clearly established.[13] Notice of the Attorney General's determination that an application should not be approved must indicate what modifications, if any, should be made in the application needed to make it meet with the Attorney General's approval.[14] The official receiving the Attorney General's notice of modifications which would make the application acceptable must modify the application if the official deems such modifications warranted. Except in cases of disability or other unavailability, the responsibility to supervise any such modifications is also a non-delegable responsibility.[15]

If a judge makes the finding required under 50 U.S.C. § 1805(a), then he or she must enter an ex parte order as requested or as modified approving the electronic surveillance. The necessary findings must include that:

---

[9] For a list of those covered in 50 U.S.C. § 1801(b)(2), see footnote 14, *supra*.
[10] 50 U.S.C. § 1804(e)(1)(A).
[11] 50 U.S.C. § 1804(e)(1)(B).
[12] 50 U.S.C. § 1804(e)(1)(C).
[13] 50 U.S.C. § 1804(e)(2)(A).
[14] 50 U.S.C. § 1804(e)(2)(B).
[15] 50 U.S.C. § 1804(e)(2)(C).

(1) the President has authorized the Attorney General to approve applications for electronic surveillance for foreign intelligence information;
(2) the application has been made by a Federal officer and approved by the Attorney General;
(3) on the basis of the facts submitted by the applicant there is probable cause to believe that –
    (A) the target of the electronic surveillance is a foreign power or an agent of a foreign power: *Provided*, That no United States person may be considered a foreign power or an agent of a foreign power solely upon the basis of activities protected by the first amendment to the Constitution of the United States; and
    (B) each of the facilities or places at which the electronic surveillance is directed is being used, or is about to be used, by a foreign power or an agent of a foreign power;
(4) the proposed minimization procedures meet the definition of minimization procedures under section 1801(h) of this title; and
(5) the application which has been filed contains all statements and certifications required by section 1804 of this title and, if the target is a United States person, the certification or certifications are not clearly erroneous on the basis of the statement made under section 1804(a)(7)(E) of this title and any other information furnished under section 1804(d) of this title.

In making a probable cause determination under 50 U.S.C. § 1805(a)(3), the judge may consider past activities of the target as well as facts and circumstances relating to the target's current or future activities.[16] An order approving an electronic surveillance under Section 1805(c) must:

(1) specify –
    (A) the identity, if known, or a description of the target of the electronic surveillance;
    (B) the nature and location of each of the facilities or places at which the electronic surveillance will be directed, *if known*;[17]
    (C) the type of information sought to be acquired and the type of communications or activities to be subjected to the surveillance;
    (D) the means by which the electronic surveillance will be effected and whether physical entry will be used to effect the surveillance;
    (E) the period of time during which the electronic surveillance is approved; and

[16] 50 U.S.C. § 1805(b).

[17] Section 314(a)(2)(A) of H. Rept. 107-328, the conference report on the Intelligence Authorization Act for Fiscal Year 2002, to accompany H.R. 2883, added "if known" to the end of Section 1905(c)(1)(B) before the semi-colon. The conference version of the bill passed both the House and the Senate, and was signed by the President on December 28, 2001.

(F) whenever more than one electronic, mechanical, or other surveillance device is to be used under the order, the authorized coverage of the device involved and what minimization procedures shall apply to information subject to acquisition by each device; and

(2) direct –

(A) that the minimization procedures be followed;

(B) that, upon the request of the applicant a specified communication or other common carrier, landlord, custodian, or other specified person, *or in circumstances where the Court finds that the actions of the target of the application may have the effect of thwarting the identification of a specified person, such other persons*, furnish the applicant forthwith all information, facilities, or technical assistance necessary to accomplish the electronic surveillance in such a manner as will protect its secrecy and produce a minimum of interference with the services that such carrier, landlord, custodian, or other person is providing that target of electronic surveillance;

(C) that such carrier, landlord, custodian, or other person maintain under security procedures approved by the Attorney General and the Director of Central Intelligence any records concerning the surveillance of the aid furnished that such person wishes to retain; and

(D) that the applicant compensate, at the prevailing rate, such carrier, landlord, custodian, or other person for furnishing such aid.[18]

The italicized portions of Section 1805(c)(1)(B) and Section 1805(c)(2)(B) reflect changes, added by P.L. 107-108 and P.L. 107-56 respectively, intended to provide authority for "multipoint" or "roving" electronic surveillance where the actions of the target of the surveillance, such as switching phones and locations repeatedly, may thwart that surveillance. The Conference Report on H.R. 2338, the Intelligence Authorization Act for Fiscal year 2002, H. Rept. 107-328, at page 24, provided the following explanation of these changes:

> The multipoint wiretap amendment to FISA in the USA PATRIOT Act (section 206) allows the FISA court to issue generic orders of assistance to any communications provider or similar person, instead of to a particular communications provider. This change permits the Government to

---

[18] 50 U.S.C. § 1805(c). The italics in 50 U.S.C. § 1805(c)(2)(B), above, indicates new language added by Section 206 of P.L. 107-56. Where circumstances suggest that a target's actions may prevent identification of a specified person, this new language appears to permit the Foreign Intelligence Surveillance Court to require a service provider, other common carrier, landlord, custodian or other persons to provide necessary assistance to the applicant for a FISA order for electronic surveillance. The heading to Section 6 of P.L. 107-56 refers to this as "roving surveillance authority." H. Rept. 107-328 calls this a "multipoint" wiretap. *Intelligence Authorization Act for Fiscal Year 2002*, 107th Cong., 1st Sess., H. Rept. 107-328, Conference Report, at 24 (Dec. 6, 2001).

> implement new surveillance immediately if the FISA target changes providers in an effort to thwart surveillance. The amendment was directed at persons who, for example, attempt to defeat surveillance by changing wireless telephone providers or using pay phones.
>
> Currently, FISA requires the court to "specify" the "nature and location of each of the facilities or places at which the electronic surveillance will be directed." 50 U.S.C. § 105(c)(1)(B). Obviously, in certain situations under current law, such a specification is limited. For example, a wireless phone has no fixed location and electronic mail may be accessed from any number of locations.
>
> To avoid any ambiguity and clarify Congress' intent, the conferees agreed to a provision which adds the phrase, "if known," to the end of 50 U.S.C. § 1805(c)(1)(B). The "if known" language, which follows the model of 50 U.S.C. § 1805(c)(1)(A), is designed to avoid any uncertainty about the kind of specification required in a multipoint wiretap case, where the facility to be monitored is typically not known in advance.

If the target of the electronic surveillance is a foreign power and each of the facilities or places at which the surveillance is directed is owned, leased, or exclusively used by that foreign power, the order does not need to include the information covered by Section 1805(c)(1)(C), (D), and (F), but must generally describe the information sought, the communications or activities subject to surveillance, the type of electronic surveillance used, and whether physical entry is needed. 50 U.S.C. § 1805(d).

Such an order may approve an electronic surveillance for the period of time necessary to achieve its purpose or for ninety days, whichever is less, unless the order is targeted against a foreign power. In that event, the order shall approve an electronic surveillance for the period specified in the order or for one year, whichever is less. An order under FISA for surveillance targeted against an agent of a foreign power who acts in the United States as an officer or employee of a foreign power, or as a member of a group engaged in international terrorism or activities in preparation therefor, may be for the period specified in the order or 120 days, whichever is less.[19] Generally, upon application for an extension, a court may grant an extension of an order on the same basis as an original order. An extension must include new findings made in the same manner as that required for the original order. However, an extension of an order for a surveillance targeting a foreign power that is not a United States person may be for a period of up to one year if the judge finds probable cause to believe that no communication of any individual United States person will be acquired during the period involved. In addition, an extension of an order for surveillance targeted at an

---

[19] 50 U.S.C. § 1805(e)(1)(B), as added by Section 207 of P.L. 107-56.

agent of a foreign power who acts in the United States as an officer or employees of a foreign power or as a member of a group engaged in international terrorism or activities in preparation therefore may be extended to a period not exceeding one year. 50 U.S.C. § 1805(e)(2)(A) and (B).[20]

Emergency situations are addressed in 50 U.S.C. § 1805(f).[21] Notwithstanding other provisions of this subchapter, if the Attorney General reasonably determines that an emergency situation exists with respect to the employment of electronic surveillance to obtain foreign intelligence information before an order authorizing such surveillance can with due diligence be obtained and that the factual basis for issuance of an order under this subchapter to approve such surveillance exists, he may authorize electronic surveillance if specified steps are taken. At the time of the Attorney General's emergency authorization, he or his designee must inform an FSIC judge that the decision to employ emergency electronic surveillance

---

[20] Section 207 of P.L. 107-56 appears to have included a mistaken citation here, referring to 50 U.S.C. § *1805(d)(2)* instead of 50 U.S.C. § *1805(e)(2)* (emphasis added). The amending statutory language discussed above appears to reflect an intended change to subsection 1805(e)(2), as there is no existing statutory language readily susceptible to such an amendment in subsection 1805(d)(2). Section 314(c)(1) of P.L. 107-108, the conference version of H.R. 2883, in H. Rept. 107-328, corrected the apparent error from P.L. 107-56, Section 207, so that the reference is now to 50 U.S.C. § 1805(e)(2). The conference version of H.R. 2883 was signed into law by the President on December 28, 2001.

[21] 50 U.S.C. § 1805(g) authorizes officers, employees, or agents of the United States to conduct electronic surveillance in the normal course of their official duties to test electronic equipment, determine the existence and capability of equipment used for unauthorized electronic surveillance, or to train intelligence personnel in the use of electronic surveillance equipment. Under 50 U.S.C. § 1805(h), the certifications of the Attorney General pursuant to 50 U.S.C. § 1802(a) and applications made and orders granted for electronic surveillance under FISA must be retained for at least 10 years.

Section 225 of P.L. 107-56 appears to crate a second subsection 1805(h), which precludes any cause of action in any court "against any provider of a wire or electronic communication service, landlord, custodian, or other person (including any officer, employee, agent or other specified person thereof) that furnishes any information, facilities, or technical assistance in accordance with a court order or request for emergency assistance" under FISA. This immunity provision is included in 50 U.S.C. § 1805, and was denominated "Immunity for Compliance with FISA Wiretap" in Section 225 of the USA PATRIOT Act, both facts which might lead one to conclude that it applied only to electronic surveillance under FISA. However, in H. Rept. 107-328, the conference report accompanying H.R. 2883, which became P.L. 107-108, the conferees expressed the view that "the text of section 225 refers to curt orders and requests for emergency assistance 'under this Act,' which makes clear that it applies to physical searches (and pen-trap requests – for which there already exists an immunity provision, 50 U.S.C. § 1842(f) – and subpoenas) as well as electronic surveillance." *Id.* at 25.

Section 314(a)(2)(C) of P.L. 107-108, the conference report version of H.R. 2883, in H. Rept. 107-328, changed subsection (h), which was added to 50 U.S.C. § 1805 by Section 225 of P.L. 107-56, to subsection (i). In addition, Section 314(a)(2)(D) of the conference report version of H.R. 2883 added "for electronic surveillance of physical search" to the has been made. An application for a court order under Section 1804 must be made to that judge as soon as practicable, but not more than 72 hours after the Attorney General authorizes such surveillance. If the Attorney General authorizes emergency electronic surveillance, he must require compliance with the minimization procedures required for the issuance of a judicial order under this subchapter. Absent a judicial order approving the emergency electronic surveillance, the surveillance must terminate when the information sought is obtained, when the application for the order is denied, or after 72 hours from the time of the Attorney General's authorization, whichever is earliest.[22] If no judicial order approving the surveillance is issued, the information garnered may not be received in evidence or otherwise disclosed in any court proceeding, or proceeding in or before any grand jury, department, office, agency, regulatory body, legislative committee, or other authority of the United States, a State, or political subdivision thereof. No information concerning any United States person acquired through such surveillance may be disclosed by any Federal officer or employee without the consent of that person, unless the Attorney General approves of such disclosure or use where the information indicates a threat of death or serious bodily harm to any person.[23]

---

end of the newly designated 50 U.S.C. § 1805(i) before the final period. The measure was signed into law by the President on December 28, 2001.

[22] Section 314(a)(2)(B) of the conference report version of H.R. 2883, the Intelligence Authorization Act for Fiscal Year 2002, H. Rept. 107-328, replaced 24 hours with 72 hours in each place that it appears in 50 U.S.C. § 1805(f). The measure was forwarded to the President for his signature on December 8, 2001, and signed into law on December 28, 2001, as P.L. 107-108.

[23] Some of the provisions dealing with interception of wire, oral, or electronic communications in the context of criminal law investigation, 18 U.S.C. §§ 2510 *et seq*., may also be worthy of note. With certain exceptions, these provisions, among other things, prohibit any person from engaging in intentional interception; attempted interception; or procuring others to intercept or endeavor to intercept wire, oral, or electronic communication; or intentional disclosure; attempting to disclose; using or endeavoring to use the contents of a wire, oral or electronic communication, knowing or having reason to know that the information was obtained by such an unlawful interception. 18 U.S.C. § 2511. "Person" is defined in 18 U.S.C. § 2510(6) to include "any employee, or agent of the United States or any State or political subdivision thereof, and any individual, partnership, association, joint stock company, trust, or corporation." Among the exceptions to Section 2511 are two of particular note:

> (2)(e) Notwithstanding any other provision of this title or section 705 or 706 of the Communications Act of 1934, it shall not be unlawful for an officer, employee, or agent of the United States in the normal course of his official duty to conduct electronic surveillance, as defined in section 101 of the Foreign Intelligence Surveillance Act of 1978, as authorized by that Act.
>
> (2)(f) Nothing contained in this chapter or chapter 121, or section 705 of the Communications Act of 1934, shall be deemed to affect the acquisition by the United States Government of foreign

> intelligence information from international or foreign communications, or foreign intelligence activities conducted in accordance with otherwise applicable Federal law involving a foreign electronic communications system, utilizing a means other than electronic surveillance as defined in section 101 of the Foreign Intelligence Surveillance Act of 1978, and procedures in this chapter and the Foreign Intelligence Surveillance Act of 1978 shall be the exclusive means by which electronic surveillance, as defined in section 101 of such Act, and the interception of domestic wire and oral communications may be conducted.

Among other things, Section 2512 prohibits any person from intentionally manufacturing, assembling, possessing, or selling any electronic, mechanical, or other device, knowing that its design renders it primarily useful for the purpose of the surreptitious interception of wire, oral, or electronic communications and that such device or any component thereof has been or will be sent through the mail or transported in interstate or foreign commerce. It also prohibits any person from intentionally sending such a device through the mail or sending or carrying such a device in interstate or foreign commerce, knowing that such surreptitious interception is its primary purpose. Similarly, intentionally advertising such a device, knowing or having reason to know that the advertisement will be sent through the mail or transported in interstate or foreign commerce is foreclosed. Again an exception to these general prohibitions in Section 2512 may be of particular interest:

> (2) It shall not be unlawful under this section for –
>
> (a) ...
>
> (b) an officer, agent, or employee of, or a person under contract with, the United States...in the normal course of the activities of the United States..., to send through the mail, send or carry in interstate or foreign commerce, or manufacture, assemble, possess, or sell any electronic, mechanical, or other device knowing or having reason to know that the design of such device renders it primarily useful for the purpose of the surreptitious interception of wire, oral, or electronic communications.

In addition, Section 107 of the Electronic Communications Privacy Act of 1986, P.L. 99-508, 100 Stat. 1858, October 21, 1986, [which enacted 18 U.S.C. §§ 1367, 2621, 2701 to 2711, 3117, and 3121 to 3126; and amended 18 U.S.C. §§ 2232, 2511-2513, and 2516-2520], provided generally that, "[n]othing in this Act or the amendments made by this Act constitutes authority for the conduct of any intelligence activity." It also stated:

> (b) Certain Activities Under Procedures Approved by the Attorney General. – Nothing in chapter 119 [interception of wire, oral or electronic communications] or chapter 121 [stored wire and electronic communications and transactional records access] of title 18, United States Code, shall affect the conduct, by officers or employees of the United States Government in accordance with other applicable Federal law, under procedures approved by the Attorney General of activities intended to –
>
> (1) intercept encrypted or other official communications of United States executive branch entities or United States Government contractors for communications security purposes;
>
> (2) intercept radio communications transmitted between or among foreign powers or agents of a foreign power as defined by the Foreign Intelligence Surveillance Act of 1978 [50 U.S.C. § 1801 et seq.]; or

The uses to which information gathered under FISA may be put are addressed under 50 U.S.C. § 1806.[24] Under these provisions, disclosure,

---

> (3) access an electronic communication system used exclusively by a foreign power or agent of a foreign power as defined by the Foreign Intelligence Surveillance Act of 1978 [50 U.S.C. § 1801 et seq.].

In addition, Chapter 121 of title 18 of the United States Code deals with stored wire and electronic communications and transactional records. Under 18 U.S.C. § 2701, intentionally accessing without authorization a facility through which an electronic communication service is provided, or intentionally exceeding an authorization to access such a facility and thereby obtaining, altering, or preventing authorized access to a wire or electronic communication while it is in electronic storage in such system is prohibited. Upon compliance with statutory requirements in 18 U.S.C. § 2709, the Director of the FBI or his designee in a position not lower than deputy Assistant Director may seek access to telephone toll and transactional records for foreign counterintelligence purposes. The FBI may disseminate information and records obtained under this section only as provided in guidelines approved by the Attorney General for foreign intelligence collection and foreign counterintelligence investigations conducted by the FBI, and, "with respect to dissemination to an agency of the United States, only if such information is clearly relevant to the authorized responsibilities of such agency." 18 U.S.C. § 2709(d).

[24] The provisions of Section 1806 are as follows:

> (a) Compliance with minimization procedures; privileged communications; lawful purposes
>
> Information acquired from an electronic surveillance conducted pursuant to this subchapter concerning any United States person may be used and disclosed by Federal officers and employees without the consent of the United States person only in accordance with the minimization procedures required by this subchapter. No otherwise privileged communication obtained in accordance with or in violation of this subchapter shall lose its privileged character. No information acquired from an electronic surveillance pursuant to this subchapter may be used or disclosed by Federal officers or employees except for lawful purposes.
>
> (b) Statement for disclosure
>
> No information acquired pursuant to this subchapter shall be disclosed for law enforcement purposes unless such disclosure is accompanied by a statement that such information, or any information derived therefrom, may only be used in a criminal proceeding with the advance authorization of the Attorney General.
>
> (c) Notification by United States
>
> Whenever the Government intends to enter into evidence or otherwise use or disclose in any trial, hearing, or other proceeding in or before any court, department, officer, agency, regulatory body, or other authority of the United States, against an aggrieved person, any information obtained or derived from an electronic surveillance of that aggrieved person pursuant to the authority of this subchapter, the Government shall, prior to the trial, hearing, or other proceeding or at a reasonable time prior to an effort to so disclose or so use that information or submit it in evidence, notify the aggrieved person and the court or other authority in which the information is to be disclosed or used that the Government intends to so disclose or so use such information.
>
> (d) Notification by States or political subdivisions

Whenever any State or political subdivision thereof intends to enter into evidence or otherwise use or disclose in any trial, hearing, or other proceeding in or before any court, department, officer, agency, regulatory body, or other authority of a State or a political subdivision thereof, against an aggrieved person any information obtained or derived from an electronic surveillance of that aggrieved person pursuant to the authority of this subchapter, the State or political subdivision thereof intends to so disclose or so use such information.

(e) Motion to suppress

Any person against whom evidence obtained or derived from an electronic surveillance to which he is an aggrieved person is to be, or has been, introduced or otherwise used or disclosed in any trial, hearing, or other proceeding in or before any court, department, officer, agency, regulatory body, or other authority of the United States, a State, or a political subdivision thereof, may move to suppress the evidence obtained or derived from such electronic surveillance on the grounds that –

(1) the information was unlawfully acquired; or

(2) the surveillance was not made in conformity with an order of authorization or approval.

Such a motion shall be made before the trial, hearing, or other proceeding unless there was no opportunity to make such a motion or the person was not aware of the grounds of the motion.

(f) In camera and ex parte review by district court

Whenever a court or other authority is notified pursuant to subsection (c) or (d) of this section, or whenever a motion is made pursuant to subsection (e) of this section, or whenever any motion or request is made by an aggrieved person pursuant to any other statute or rule of the United States or any State before any court or other authority of the United States or any State to discover or obtain applications or orders or other materials relating to electronic surveillance or to discover, obtain, or suppress evidence or information obtained or derived from electronic surveillance under this chapter, the United States district court or, where the motion is made before another authority, the United States district court in the same district as the authority, shall, notwithstanding any other law, if the Attorney General files an affidavit under oath that disclosure of an adversary haring would harm the national security of the United States, review in camera and ex parte the application, order, and such other materials relating to the surveillance as may be necessary to determine whether the surveillance of the aggrieved person was lawfully authorized and conducted. In making this determination, the court may disclose to the aggrieved person, under appropriate security procedures and protective orders, portions of the application, order, or other materials relating to the surveillance only where such disclosure is necessary to make an accurate determination of the legality of the surveillance.

(g) Suppression of evidence; denial of motion

If the United States district court pursuant to subsection (f) of this section determines that the surveillance was not lawfully authorized or conducted, it shall, in accordance with the requirements of law, suppress the evidence which was unlawfully obtained or derived from electronic surveillance of the aggrieved person or otherwise grant the motion of the aggrieved person. If the court determines that the surveillance was lawfully authorized and conducted, it shall deny the motion of the aggrieved person except to the extent that due process requires discovery or disclosure.

(h) Finality of orders

Orders granting motions or requests under subsection (g) of this section, decisions under this section that electronic surveillance was not lawfully authorized or conducted, and orders of the United States district court requiring review or granting disclosure of applications, orders, or other materials relating to a surveillance shall be final orders and binding upon all courts of the Untied States and the several States except a United States court of appeals and the Supreme Court.

(i) Destruction of unintentionally acquired information

In circumstances involving the unintentional acquisition by an electronic, mechanical, or other surveillance device of the contents of any radio communication, under circumstances in which a person has a reasonable expectation of privacy and a warrant would be required for law enforcement purposes, and if both the sender and all intended recipients are located within the United States, unless the Attorney General determines that the contents indicate a threat of death or serious bodily hard to any person.

(j) Notification of emergency employment of electronic surveillance; contents; postponement, suspension or elimination

If an emergency employment of electronic surveillance is authorized under section 1805(e) of this title and a subsequent order approving the surveillance is not obtained, the judge shall cause to be served on any United States person named in the application or on such other United States persons subject to electronic surveillance as the judge may determine in his discretion it is in the interest of justice to serve, notice of –

(1) the fact of the application;

(2) the period of the surveillance; and

(3) the fact that during the period information was or was not obtained.

On an ex parte showing of good cause to the judge the serving of the notice required by this subsection may be postponed or suspended for a period not to exceed ninety days. Thereafter, on a further ex parte showing of good cause, the court shall forgo ordering the serving of the notice required under this subsection.

(k)(1) Federal officers who conduct electronic surveillance to acquire foreign intelligence information under this title may consult with Federal law enforcement officers to coordinate efforts to investigate or protect against –

(A) actual or potential attack or other grave hostile acts of a foreign power or an agent of a foreign power.

(B) sabotage or international terrorism by a foreign power or an agent of a foreign power; or

(C) clandestine intelligence activities by an intelligence service or network of a foreign power or by an agent of a foreign power.

(2) Coordination authorized under paragraph (1) shall not preclude the certification required by section 104(a)(7)(B) [50 U.S.C. § 1804(a)(7)(B) (referring to a certification by the Assistant to the President for National Security Affairs or other designated certifying authority "that a significant purpose of the surveillance is to obtain foreign intelligence information")] or the entry of an order under section 105 [50 U.S.C. § 1805].

without the consent of the person involved, of information lawfully acquired under FISA which concerns a United States person must be in compliance with the statutorily mandated minimization procedures. Communications which were privileged when intercepted remain privileged. Where information acquired under FISA is disclosed for law enforcement purposes, neither that information nor any information derived therefrom may be used in a criminal proceeding without prior authorization of the Attorney General. If the United States Government intends to disclose information acquired under FISA or derived therefrom in any proceeding before a court, department, officer regulatory body or other authority of the United States against an aggrieved person,[25] then the Government must give prior notice of its intent to disclose to the aggrieved person and to the court or other authority involved. Similarly, a State or political subdivision of a State that intends to disclose such information against an aggrieved person in a proceeding before a State or local authority must give prior notice of its intent to the aggrieved person, the court or other authority, and the Attorney General.

Section 1806 also sets out in camera and ex parte district court review procedures to be followed where such notification is received, or where the aggrieved person seeks to discover or obtain orders or applications relating to FISA electronic surveillance, or to discover, obtain, or suppress evidence of information obtained or derived from the electronic surveillance, and the Attorney General files an affidavit under oath that such disclosure would harm U.S. national security. The focus of this review would be to determine whether the surveillance was lawfully conducted and authorized. Only where needed to make an accurate determination of these issues does the section permit the court to disclose to the aggrieved person, under appropriate security measures and protective orders, parts of the application, order, or other materials related to the surveillance. If, as a result of its review, the district court determines that the surveillance was unlawful, the resulting evidence must be suppressed.[26] If the surveillance was lawfully authorized

Subsection 1806(k) was added by Section 504 of P.L. 107-56. The term "aggrieved person," as used in connection with electronic surveillance under FISA, is defined under 50 U.S.C. § 1801(k) to mean "a person who is the target of an electronic surveillance or any other person whose communications or activities were subject to electronic surveillance."

[25] For the definition of "aggrieved person" as that term is used with respect to targets of electronic surveillance under IFSA, see fn. 35, *supra*.

[26] *But see, United States v. Thomson*, 752 F. Supp. 75, 77 (W.D. N.Y. 1990), stating that,

> If the Court determines that the surveillance was unlawfully authorized or conducted, it must order disclosure of the FISA material. 50 U.S.C. § 1806(g).... In *United States v. Belfield*, 692 F.2d 141 (D.C. Cir. 1982),

and conducted, the motion of the aggrieved person must be denied except to the extent that due process requires discovery or disclosure. Resultant court orders granting motions or requests of the aggrieved person for a determination that the surveillance was not lawfully conducted or authorized and court orders requiring review or granting disclosure are final orders binding on all Federal and State courts except a U.S. Court of Appeals and the U.S. Supreme Court.

If the contents of any radio communication are unintentionally acquired by an electronic, mechanical, or other surveillance device in circumstances where there is a reasonable expectation of privacy and where a warrant would be required if the surveillance were to be pursued for law enforcement purposes, then the contents must be destroyed when recognized, unless the Attorney General finds that the contents indicate a threat of death or serious bodily harm to any person.

As noted above, Section 1805 provides for emergency electronic surveillance in limited circumstances, and requires the subsequent prompt filing of an application for court authorization to the FISC in such a situation. Under Section 1806, if the application is unsuccessful in obtaining

---

the court stated that: "even when the government has purported not to be offering any evidence obtained or derived from the electronic surveillance, a criminal defendant may claim that he has been the victim of an illegal surveillance and seek discovery of the FISA surveillance material to ensure that no fruits thereof are being used against him." Id. at 146.

It may be noted that the Section 1806(g) does not state that a court must order disclosure of the FISA material if the court finds that the FISA electronic surveillance was unlawfully authorized or conducted. Rather, the provision in question states in pertinent part that, "If the United States district court pursuant to subsection (f) of this section determines that the surveillance was not lawfully authorized or conducted, it shall, in accordance with the requirements of law, suppress the evidence which was unlawfully obtained or derived from electronic surveillance of the aggrieved person or otherwise grant the motion of the aggrieved person...." While a district court will normally consider in camera and ex parte a motion to suppress under Subsection 1806(e) or other statute or rule to discover, disclose, or suppress information relating to a FISA electronic surveillance, Subsection 1806(f) does permit a district court, in determining the legality of a FISA electronic surveillance, to disclose to the aggrieved person, under appropriate security procedures and protective orders, portions of the application, order or other materials relating to the surveillance only to the extent necessary to make an accurate determination of the legality of the surveillance. *Belfield* indicated that a criminal defendant may seek to discover FISA surveillance material to ensure that no fruits of an illegal surveillance are being used against him, but it appears to stop short of saying that in every instance where the court finds an illegal surveillance disclosure must be forthcoming. "The language of section 1806(f) clearly anticipates that ex parte, in camera determination is to be the rule. Disclosure and an adversary hearing are the exception, occurring only when necessary." *Belfield, supra*, 692 F.2d at 147. *See also, United States v. Squillacote*, 221 F.3d 542, 552-554 (4th Cir. 2000), *cert. denied*, ____ U.S. ____, 2001 U.S. LEXIS 2915 (April 16, 2001).

court approval for the surveillance, notice must be served upon any United States person named in the application and such other U.S. persons subject to electronic surveillance as the judge determines, in the exercise of his discretion, is in the interests of justice. This notice includes the fact of the application, the period of surveillance, and the fact that information was or was not obtained during this period. Section 1806 permits postponement or suspension of service of notice for up to ninety days upon ex parte good cause shown. Upon a further ex parte showing of good cause thereafter, the court will forego ordering such service of notice.[27]

P.L. 107-56, Section 504, added a new subsection 1896(k)(1). Under this new subsection, federal officers who conduct electronic surveillance to acquire foreign intelligence under FISA are permitted to consult with Federal law enforcement officers to coordinate investigative efforts or to protect against –

> (A) actual or potential attack or other grave hostile acts of a foreign power or an agent of a foreign power;
> (B) sabotage or international terrorism by a foreign power or an agent of a foreign power; or
> (C) clandestine intelligence activities by an intelligence service or network of a foreign power or by an agent of a foreign power.

This new subsection indicates further that such coordination would not preclude certification as required by 50 U.S.C. § 1804(a)(7)(B) or entry of a court order under 50 U.S.C. § 1805.

Reporting requirements are included in Sections 1807 and 1808. Under Section 1807, each year in April, the Attorney General is directed to transmit to the Administrative Office of the United States Courts and to the Congress a report covering the total number of applications made for orders and extensions of orders approving electronic surveillance under FISA during the

---

[27] *Cf.*, *United States Attorney's Manual*, §§ 1-2.106 (Office of Intelligence Policy and Review organization and functions). This section indicates, in part, that the office of Intelligence Policy and Review

> ...prepares certifications and applications for electronic surveillance under the Foreign Intelligence Surveillance Act, 50 U.S.C. § 1801 et seq., and represents the United States before the United States Foreign Intelligence Surveillance Court. It processes requests for Attorney General Authority to use FISA material in adjudicatory proceedings and assists in responding to challenges to the legality of FISA surveillances.

See also, 28 C.F.R. § 0.33 (functions of the Counsel for Intelligence Policy); *United States Attorneys' Criminal Resource Manual*, §§ 1073 (FISA-50 U.S.C. § 1809) and 1075 (elements of the offense under 50 U.S.C. § 1809(a); *cf.*, *United States Attorney's Manual* § 9-7.301 (consensual monitoring in the context of electronic surveillance).

previous year, and the total number of orders and extensions granted, modified, or denied during that time period. Section 1808(a) requires the Attorney General to fully inform the House Permanent Select Committee on Intelligence and the Senate Select Committee on Intelligence semiannually about all electronic surveillance under FISA.[28] Each such report must contain a description of each criminal case in which information acquired under FISA "has been passed for law enforcement purposes" during the period covered by the report, and each criminal case in which information acquired under FISA has been authorized to be used at trial during the reporting period.[29]

Section 1809 provides criminal sanctions for intentionally engaging in electronic surveillance under color of law except as authorized by statute; or for disclosing or using information obtained under color of law by electronic surveillance, knowing or having reason to know that surveillance was not authorized by statute.[30] The provision makes it a defense to prosecution under this subsection if the defendant is a law enforcement officer or investigative officer in the course of his official duties and the electronic surveillance was authorized by and conducted under a search warrant or court order of a court of competent jurisdiction. Section 1809 provides for Federal jurisdiction over such an offense if the defendant is a Federal officer or employee at the time of the offense. Civil liability is also provided for under Section 1810, where an aggrieved person, who is neither a foreign

---

[28] Subsection 1808(b) directed these committees to report annually for five years after the date of enactment to the House and the Senate respectively concerning implementation of FISA, including any recommendations for amendment, repeal, or continuation without amendment. P.L. 106-567, Title VI, Sec. 604(b) (Dec. 27, 2000), 114 Stat. 2853, required the Attorney General to submit to the Senate Select Committee on Intelligence, the Senate Judiciary Committee, the House Permanent Select Committee on Intelligence, and the House Judiciary Committee a report on the authorities and procedures utilized by the Department of Justice to determine whether or not to disclose information acquired under FISA for law enforcement purposes. 50 U.S.C. § 1806 note.

[29] 50 U.S.C. § 1808(a)(2).

[30] Section 1075 of the *United States Attorneys' Criminal Resource Manual* indicates that Section 1809(a) "reaches two distinct acts: (1) engaging in unauthorized electronic surveillance under color of law; and (2) using or disclosing information obtained under color of law through unauthorized electronic surveillance. Each offense involves an "intentional" state of mind and unauthorized "electronic surveillance." Section 1075 further notes:

> Even though none of these elements mentions foreign intelligence, one court has explained that "the FISA applies only to surveillance designed to gather information relevant to foreign intelligence." *United States v. Koyomejian*, 970 F.2d 536, 540 (9th Cir. 1992) (en banc), cert denied, 506 U.S. 1005 (1992). In fact, all applications for an order from the Foreign Intelligence Surveillance Court require a certification from a presidentially designated official that the purpose of the surveillance is to obtain foreign intelligence. 50 U.S.C. § 1804(a)(7).

power nor an agent of a foreign power, has been subjected to electronic surveillance, or where information gathered by electronic surveillance about an aggrieved person has been disclosed or used in violation of Section 1809.

Finally, Section 1811 provides that, notwithstanding any other law, the President, through the Attorney General, may authorize electronic surveillance without a court order to acquire foreign intelligence information for up to 15 calendar days following a declaration of war by Congress.

Physical Searches for Foreign Intelligence Gathering Purposes

Physical searches for foreign intelligence purposes are addressed in 50 U.S.C. § 1821 *et seq.*[31] While tailored for physical searches, the provisions in many respects follow a pattern similar to that created for electronic surveillance. The definitions from 50 U.S.C. § 1801 for the terms "foreign power," "agent of a foreign power," "international terrorism," "sabotage," "foreign intelligence information," "Attorney General," "United States person," "United States," "person," and "State" also apply to foreign intelligence physical searches except where specifically provided otherwise. A "physical search" under this title means:

> any physical intrusion within the United States into premises or property (including examination of the interior of property by technical means) that is intended to result in seizure, reproduction, inspection, or alteration of information, material, or property, under circumstances in which a person has a reasonable expectation of privacy and a warrant would be required for law enforcement purposes, but does not include (A) "electronic surveillance", as defined in section 1801(f) of this title [50 U.S.C.], or (B) the acquisition by the United States Government of foreign intelligence information from international or foreign communications, or foreign intelligence activities conducted in accordance with otherwise applicable Federal law involving a foreign electronic communications system, utilizing a means other than electronic surveillance as defined in section 1801(f) of this title.[32]

Minimization procedures also apply to physical searches for foreign intelligence purposes. Those defined under 50 U.S.C. § 1821(4) are tailored

---

[31] The physical search provisions of FISA were added as Title III of that Act by P.L. 103-359, Title VIII, on October 14, 1994; 108 Stat. 3443. Some of these provisions were subsequently amended by P.L. 106-567, Title VI, on December 27, 2000, 114 Stat. 2852-53; and by P.L. 107-56.

[32] 50 U.S.C. § 1821(5).

to such physical searches, and like those applicable to electronic surveillance under 50 U.S.C. § 1801(h), these procedures are designed to minimize acquisition and retention, and to prohibit dissemination of nonpublicly available information concerning unconsenting U.S. persons, consistent with the needs of the United States to obtain, produce and disseminate foreign intelligence.[33]

Under 50 U.S.C. § 1822, the President, acting through the Attorney General may authorize physical searches to acquire foreign intelligence information without a court order for up to one year if the Attorney General certifies under oath that the search is solely directed at premises, property, information or materials owned by or under the open and exclusive control of a foreign power or powers.[34] For these purposes, "foreign power or powers" means a foreign government or component of a foreign

---

[33] Specifically, 50 U.S.C. § 1821(4) defines "minimization procedures" with respect to physical search to mean:

> (A) specific procedures, which shall be adopted by the Attorney General, that are reasonably designed in light of the purposes and technique of the particular physical search, to minimize the acquisition and retention, and prohibit the dissemination, of nonpublicly available information concerning unconsenting United States persons consistent with the need of the United States to obtain, produce, and disseminate foreign intelligence information;
> (B) procedures that require that nonpublicly available information, which is not foreign intelligence information, as defined in section 1801(e)(1) of this title, shall not be disseminated in a manner that identifies any United States person, without such person'' consent, unless such person'' identity is necessary to understand such foreign intelligence information or assess its importance;
> (C) notwithstanding subparagraphs (A) and (B), procedures that allow for the retention and dissemination of information that is evidence of a crime which has been, is being, or is about to be committed and that is to be retained or disseminated for law enforcement purposes; and
> (D) notwithstanding subparagraphs (A), (B), and (C), with respect to any physical search approved pursuant to section 1822(a) of this title, procedures that require that no information, material, or property of a United States person shall be disclosed, disseminated, or used for any purpose or retained for longer than 72 hours, unless a court order under section 1824 of this title is obtained or unless the Attorney General determines that the information indicates a threat of death or serious bodily harm to any person.

Section 314(a)(3) of P.L. 107-108, the conference version of the Intelligence Authorization Act of 2002, H.R. 2882, from H. Rept. 107-328, changed the previous 24 hour period in the minimization procedures under 50 U.S.C. § 1821(4)(D) to a 72 hour period. The bill passed both houses of Congress and was signed by the President on December 28, 2001.

[34] The president provided such authority to the Attorney General by Executive order 12949, Section 1, 60 *Fed. Reg.* 8169 (February 9, 1995), if the Attorney General makes the certifications necessary under 50 U.S.C. § 1822(a)(1).

government, whether or not recognized by the United States, a faction of a foreign nation or nations, not substantially composed of U.S. persons; or an entity that is openly acknowledge by a foreign government or governments to be directed and controlled by such foreign government or governments.[35] In addition, the Attorney General must certify that there is no substantial likelihood that the physical search will involve the premises, information, material or property of a U.S. person, and that the proposed minimization procedures with respect to the physical search are consistent with 50 U.S.C. § 1821(4)(1)-(4).[36] Under normal circumstances, these minimization procedures and any changes to them are reported to the House Permanent Select Committee on Intelligence and the Senate Select Committee on Intelligence by the Attorney General at least 30 days before their effective date. However, if the Attorney General determines that immediate action is required, the statute mandates that he advise these committees immediately of the minimization procedures and the need for them to become effective immediately. In addition, the Attorney General must assess compliance with these minimization procedures and report such assessments to these congressional committees.

The certification of the Attorney General for a search under 50 U.S.C. § 1822 is immediately transmitted under seal to the Foreign Intelligence Surveillance Court, and maintained there under security measures established by the Chief Justice of the United States with the Attorney General's concurrence, in consultation with the Director of Central Intelligence. Such a certification remains under seal unless one of two circumstances arise: 91) either an application for a court order with respect to the physical search is made to the Foreign Intelligence Surveillance Court under 50 U.S.C. § 1821(4) (dealing with minimization procedures) and §1823 (dealing with the process by which a federal officer, with the approval of the Attorney General, may apply for an order from the FISC approving a physical search for foreign intelligence gathering purposes); or (2) the certification is needed to determine the legality of a physical search under 50 U.S.C. § 1825 (dealing with use of the information so gathered).

In connection with physical searches under 50 U.S.C. § 1822, the Attorney General may direct a landlord, custodian or other specified person to furnish all necessary assistance needed to accomplish the physical search in a way that would both protect its secrecy and minimize interference with the services such person provides the target of the search. Such person may

[35] *See* 50 U.S.C. § 1801(a)(1), (2), or (3).

[36] While this is the citation cross-referenced in Section 1822, it appears that the cross-reference should read 50 U.S.C. § 1821(4)(A)-(D).

also be directed to maintain any records regarding the search or the aid provided under security procedures approved by the Attorney General and the Director of Central Intelligence. The provision of any such aid must be compensated by the Government.[37] As in the case of applications for electronic surveillance under FISA, the Foreign Intelligence Surveillance Court (FISC) has jurisdiction to hear applications and grant applications with respect to physical searches under 50 U.S.C. § 1821 *et seq*. No FISC judge may hear an application already denied by another FISC judge. If an application for an order authorizing a physical search under FISA is denied, the judge denying the application must immediately provide a written statement of reasons for the denial. If the United States so moves, the record is then transmitted under seal to the court of review established under 50 U.S.C. § 1803(b). If the court of review determines that the application was properly denied, it, in turn, must provide a written statement of the reasons for its decision, which must be transmitted under seal to the Supreme Court upon petition for certiorari by the United States.[38] Any of the proceedings with respect to an application for a physical search under FISA must be conducted expeditiously, and the record of such proceedings must be kept under appropriate security measures.

The requirements for application for an order of a physical search under FISA are included in 50 U.S.C. § 1823. While tailored to a physical search, the requirements strongly parallel those applicable to electronic surveillance under 50 U.S.C. § 1804(a)(1)-(9).[39] Like Section 1804(a)(7)(B) with respect

---

[37] 50 U.S.C. § 1822(a)(4).

[38] 50 U.S.C. § 1822(c), (d).

[39] Each application for an order approving such a physical search, having been approved by the Attorney General based upon his understanding that the application satisfies the criteria and requirements of 50 U.S.C. § 1821 *et seq*., must be made by a Federal officer in writing upon oath or affirmation to a FISC judge. Under subsection (a) of Section 1823, the application must include:

> (1) the identity of the Federal officer making the application;
> (2) the authority conferred on the Attorney General by the President and the approval of the Attorney General to make the application;
> (3) the identity, if known, or a description of the search, and a detailed description of the premises or property to be searched and of the information, material, or property to be seized, reproduced, or altered;
> (4) a statement of the facts and circumstances relied upon by the applicant to justify the applicant's belief that –
>
> > (A) the target of the physical search is a foreign power or an agent of a foreign power;
> > (B) the premises or property to be searched contains foreign intelligence information, and
> > (C) the premises or property to be searched is owned, used, [possessed by, or is in transit to or from a foreign power or an agent of a foreign power;

to required certifications for an application for electronic surveillance under FISA, Section 1823(a)(7)(B) was amended by P.L. 107-56, Section 218, to require that the Assistant to the President for National Security Affairs or designated executive branch official[40] certify, among other things, that a significant purpose (rather than "that the purpose") of the physical search is

---

(5) a statement of the proposed minimization procedures;
(6) a statement of the nature of the foreign intelligence sought and the manner in which the physical search is to be conducted;
(7) a certification or certifications by the Assistant to the President for National Security Affairs or an executive branch official or officials designated by the President from among those executive branch officers employed in the area of national security or defense and appointed by the President, by and with the advice and consent of the Senate –
(A) that the certifying official deems the information sought to be foreign intelligence information;
(B) that a significant purpose of the search is to obtain foreign intelligence information;
(C) that such information cannot reasonably be obtained by normal investigative techniques;
(D) that designates the type of foreign intelligence information being sought according to the categories described in section 1801(e) of this title; and
(E) includes a statement explaining the basis for the certifications required by subparagraphs (C) and (D);
(8) where the physical search involves a search of the residence of a United States person, the Attorney General shall state what investigative techniques have previously been utilized to obtain the foreign intelligence information concerned and the degree to which these techniques resulted in acquiring such information; and
(9) a statement of the facts concerning all previous applications that have been made to any judge under this subchapter involving any of the persons, premises, or property specified in the application, and the action taken on each previous application.

Under Section 1823(b), the Attorney General may require any other affidavit or certification from any other officer in connection with an application for a physical search that he deems appropriate. Under Section 1823(c), the FISC judge to whom the application is submitted may also require that the applicant provide other information as needed to make the determinations necessary under 50 U.S.C. § 1824.

[40] In Section 2 of E.O. 12949, 60 *Fed. Reg.* 8169 (February 9, 1995), the President authorized the Attorney General to approve applications to the Foreign Intelligence Surveillance Court under 50 U.S.C. § 1823, to obtain court orders for physical searches for the purpose of collecting foreign intelligence information. In Section 3 of that executive order, the President designated the Secretary of State, the Secretary of Defense, the Director of Central Intelligence, the Director of the Federal Bureau for Investigation, the Deputy Secretary of State, the Deputy Secretary of Defense, and the Deputy Director of Central Intelligence to make the certifications required by 50 U.S.C. § 1823(a)(7), in support of an application for a court order for a physical search for foreign intelligence purposes. None of these officials may exercise this authority to make the appropriate certifications unless he or she is appointed by the President, with the advice and consent of the Senate.

to obtain foreign intelligence information.[41] Section 1823(d) also parallels Section 1804(e) (dealing with requirements for some applications for electronic surveillance under FISA), in that, if requested in writing by the Director of the FBI, the Secretary of Defense, the Secretary of State, or the DCI,[42] the Attorney General must personally review an application for a FISA physical search if the target is one described by Section 1801(b)(2). 50 U.S.C. § 1801(b)(2) deals with targets who knowingly engage in clandestine intelligence gathering activities involving or possibly involving violations of federal criminal laws by or on behalf of a foreign power; targets who, at the direction of n intelligence service or network of a foreign power, engage in other clandestine intelligence activities involving or potentially involving federal crimes by or on behalf of a foreign power; targets who knowingly engage in sabotage or international terrorism, activities in preparation for sabotage or international terrorism, or activities on behalf of a foreign power; targets who knowingly aid, abet, or conspire with anyone to engage in any of the previously listed categories of activities; or targets who knowingly enter the United States under false identification by or on behalf of a foreign power or who assume a false identity on behalf of a foreign power while present in the United States.[43]

Should the Attorney General, after reviewing an application, decide not to approve it, he must provide written notice of his determination to the official requesting the review of the application, setting forth any modifications needed for the Attorney General to approve it. The official so notified must supervise the making of the suggested modifications if the official deems them warranted. Unless the Attorney General or the official involved is disabled or otherwise unable to carry out his or her respective responsibilities under Section 1823, those responsibilities are non-delegable.

As in the case of the issuance of an order approving electronic surveillance under 50 U.S.C. § 1805(a), certain findings by the FISC judge are required before an order may be forthcoming authorizing a physical search for foreign intelligence information under 50 U.S.C. § 1824(a). Once an application under Section 1823 has been filed, an FISC judge must enter

---

[41] As in the case of the change from "the purpose" to "a significant purpose" in the case of electronic surveillance, the parallel language change in Section 1823 with respect to physical searches may also have the effect of blurring the distinction between physical searches for foreign intelligence purposes and those engaged in for law enforcement purposes.

[42] The authority of these officials to make such a written request is non-delegable except where such official is disabled or unavailable. Each must make provision in advance for delegation of this authority should he or she become disabled or unavailable. 50 U.S.C. § 1823(d)(1)(B) and (C).

[43] See fn. 12, *supra*.

an ex parte order, either as requested or as modified, approving the physical search if the requisite findings are made. These include findings that:

(1) the President has authorized the Attorney General to approve applications for physical searches for foreign intelligence purposes;
(2) the application has been made by a Federal officer and approved by the Attorney General;
(3) on the basis of the facts submitted by the applicant there is probably cause to believe that –
    (A) the target of the physical search is a foreign power or an agent of a foreign power, except that no United States person may be considered an agent of a foreign power solely on the basis of activities protected by the first amendment to the Constitution of the United States; and
    (B) the premises or property to be searched is owned, used, possessed by, or is in transit to or from an agent of a foreign power or a foreign power;
(4) the proposed minimization procedures meet the definition of minimization contained in this subchapter; and
(5) the application which has been filed contains all statements and certifications required by section 1823 of this title, and, if the target is a United States person, the certification or certifications are not clearly erroneous on the basis of the statement made under section 1823(a)(7)(E) of this title and any other information furnished under section 1823(c) of this title.

Like Section 1805(b) regarding electronic surveillance under FISA, a FISC judge making a probably cause determination under Section 1824 may consider the target's past activities, plus facts and circumstances pertinent to the target's present or future activities.[44]

As in the case of an order under 50 U.S.C. § 1805(c) with respect to electronic surveillance, an order granting an application for a physical search under FISA must meet statutory requirements in 50 U.S.C. § 1824(c) as to specifications and directions. An order approving a physical search much specify:

(A) the identity, if known, or a description of the target of the physical search;
(B) the nature and location of each of the premises of property to be searched;
(C) the type of information, material, or property to be seized, altered, or reproduced;
(D) a statement of the manner in which the physical search is to be conducted and, whenever more than one physical search is authorized

[44] 50 U.S.C. § 1824(b).

under the order, the authorized scope of each search and what minimization procedures shall apply to the information acquired by each search; and

(E) the period of time during which the physical searches are approved; ....

In addition, the order must direct:

(A) that the minimization procedures be followed;
(B) that, upon the request of the applicant, a specified landlord, custodian, or other specified person furnish the applicant forthwith all information, facilities, or assistance necessary to accomplish the physical search in such a manner as will protect its secrecy and produce a minimum of interference with the services that such landlord, custodian, or other person is providing to the target of the physical search;
(C) that such landlord, custodian, or other person maintain under security procedures approved by the Attorney General and the Director of Central Intelligence any records concerning the search or the aid furnished that such person wishes to retain;
(D) that the applicant compensate, at the prevailing rate, such landlord, custodian, or other person for furnishing such aid; and
(E) that the federal officer conducting the physical search promptly report to the court the circumstances and results of the physical search.[45]

Subsection 1824(d) sets the limits on the duration of orders under this section and makes provision for extensions of such orders if certain criteria are met.[46] Subsection 1824(e) deals with emergency orders for physical

---

[45] 50 U.S.C. § 1824(c)(1), (2).

[46] P.L. 107-56, Section 207(a)(2), amended 50 U.S.C. § 1824(d)(1) so that it provided:

(1) An order under this section may approve a physical search for the period necessary to achieve its purpose, or for *90* days, whichever is less, except that *(A)* an order under this section shall approve a physical search targeted against a foreign power, as defined in paragraph (1), (2), or (3) of section 101(a) [50 U.S.C. § 1801(b)(1)(A)], for the period specified in the application or for one year, whichever is less, *and (B) an order under this section for a physical search against an agent of a foreign power as defined in section 101(b)(1)(A) [50 U.S.C. § 1801(b)(1)(A)] may be for the period specified in the application or for 120 days, whichever is less.*

The language in italics reflects the changes made by P.L. 107-56. The 90 day time period reflected in the first sentence replaced earlier language which provided for forty-five days.

Section 207(b)(2) of P.L. 107-56 amended 50 U.S.C. § 1824(d)(2) to provide:

(2) Extensions of an order issued under this title [50 U.S.C. §§ 1821 et seq.] may be granted on the same basis as the original order upon an application for an extension and new findings made in the same manner as required for the original order, except that an extension of an order under this Act for a physical search targeted against a foreign power, as defined in section 101(a)(5) or (6) [50 U.S.C. § 1801(a)(5) or (6)], or against a foreign power, as defined in section 101(a)(4) [50 U.S.C. § 1801(a)(4)],

searches. It permits the Attorney General, under certain circumstances, to authorize execution of a physical search if the Attorney General or his designee informs a FISC judge that the decision to execute an emergency search has been made, and an application under 50 U.S.C. § 1821 *et seq.* is made to that judge as soon as possible, within 72 hours[47] after the Attorney General authorizes the search. The Attorney General's decision to authorize such a search must be premised upon a determination that "an emergency situation exists with respect to the execution of a physical search to obtain foreign intelligence information before an order authorizing such search can with due diligence by obtained," and "the factual basis for issuance of an order under this title [50 U.S.C. § 1821 *et seq.*] to approve such a search exists."[48] If such an emergency search is authorized by the Attorney General, he must require that the minimization procedures required for issuance of a judicial order for a physical search under 18 U.S.C. § 1821 *et seq.* be followed.[49] If there is no judicial order for such a physical search, then the search must terminate on the earliest of the date on which the information sought is obtained, the date on which the application for the order is denied, or the expiration of the 72 hour period from the Attorney General's authorization of the emergency search.[50] If an application for approval is denied or if the search is terminated and no order approving the search is issued, then neither information obtained from the search nor evidence derived from the search may be used in evidence or disclosed in any

> … trial, hearing, or other proceeding in or before any court, grand jury, department, office, agency, regulatory body, legislative committee, or other authority of the United States, a State, or political subdivision thereof, and no information concerning any United States person acquired from such

---

that is not a United States person, or *against an agent of a foreign power as defined in section 101(b)(1)(A) [50 U.S.C. § 1801(b)(1)(A)]*, may be for a period not to exceed one year if the judge finds probably cause to believe that no property of any individual United States person will be acquired during the period.

(Emphasis added.) Under subsection 1824(d)(3), the judge, at or before the end of the time approved for a physical search or for an extension, or at any time after the physical search is carried out, may review circumstances under which information regarding U.S. persons was acquired, retained, or disseminated to assess compliance with minimization techniques.

[47] Section 314(a)(4) of the Intelligence Authorization Act for Fiscal Year 2002, P.L. 107-108, amended 50 U.S.C. § 1824(e) by striking "24 hours" where it occurred and replacing it with "72 hours."

[48] 50 U.S.C. § 1824(e)(1)(A)(i) and (ii). *See* fn.58, *supra*, regarding substitution of "72 hours" for "24 hours" in Subsection 50 U.S.C. § 1824(e)(3)(C) by P.L. 107-108, Sec. 314(a)(4).

[49] 50 U.S.C. § 1824(e)(2).

[50] 50 U.S.C. § 1824(e)(3).

> search shall subsequently be used or disclosed in any other manner by Federal officers or employees without the consent of such person, except with the approval of the Attorney General, if the information indicates a threat of death or serious bodily harm to any person. A denial of the application made under this subsection may be reviewed as provided in section 302 [50 U.S.C. § 1822].[51]

Subsection 1824(f) requires retention of applications made and orders granted under 50 U.S.C. § 1821 *et seq.*, for a minimum of 10 years from the date of the application.

Like 50 U.S.C. § 1806 with respect to electronic surveillance under FISA, 50 U.S.C. § 1825 restricts and regulates the uses of information secured under a FISA physical search. Such information may only be used or disclosed by Federal officers or employees for lawful purposes. Federal officers and employees must comply with minimization procedures if they use or disclose information gathered from a physical search under FISA concerning a United States person.[52] If a physical search involving the residence of a United States person is authorized and conducted under 50 U.S.C. § 1824, and at any time thereafter the Attorney General determines that there is no national security interest in continuing to maintain the search's secrecy, the Attorney General must provide notice to the United States person whose residence was searched. This notice must include both the fact that the search pursuant to FISA was conducted and the identification of any property of that person which was seized, altered, or reproduced during the search.[53] Disclosure for law enforcement purposes of information acquired under 50 U.S.C. § 1821 *et seq.*, must be accompanied by a statement that such information and any derivative information may only be used in a criminal proceeding with advance authorization from the Attorney General.[54]

The notice requirements relevant to intended use or disclosure of information gleaned from a FISA physical search or derivative information, are similar to those applicable where disclosure or use of information garnered from electronic surveillance is intended. If the United States intends to use or disclose information gathered during or derived from a FISA physical search in a trial, hearing, or other proceeding before a court, department, officer, agency, regulatory body or other authority of the United States against an aggrieved person, the United States must first give notice to

---

[51] 50 U.S.C. § 1824(e)(4).
[52] 50 U.S.C. § 1825(a).
[53] 50 U.S.C. § 1825(b).
[54] 50 U.S.C. § 1825(c).

the aggrieved person, and the court or other authority.[55] Similarly, if a State or political subdivision of state intends to use or disclose any information obtained or derived from a FISA physical search in any trial, hearing, or other proceeding before a court, department, officer, agency, regulatory body, or other State or political subdivision against an aggrieved person, the State or locality must notify the aggrieved person, the pertinent court or other authority where the information is to be used, and the Attorney General of the United States of its intention to use of disclose the information.[56] An aggrieved person may move to suppress evidence obtained or derived from a FISA physical search on one of two grounds: that the information was unlawfully acquired; or that the physical search was not made in conformity with an order of authorization or approval. Such a motion to suppress must be made before the trial, hearing or other proceeding involved unless the aggrieved person had no opportunity to make the motion or was not aware of the grounds of the motion.[57]

In camera, ex parte review by a United States district court may be triggered by receipt of notice under Subsections 1825(d) or (e) by a court or other authority; the making of a motion to suppress by an aggrieved person under Subsection 1825(f); or the making of a motion or request by an aggrieved person under any other federal or state law or rule before any federal or state court or authority to discover or obtain applications, orders, or other materials pertaining to a physical search authorized under FISA or to discover, obtain, or suppress evidence or information obtained or derived from a FISA physical search. If the Attorney general files an affidavit under oath that disclosure or any adversary hearing would harm U.S. national security, the U.S. district court receiving notice or before whom a motion or request is pending, or, if the motion is made to another authority, the U.S. district court in the same district as that authority, shall review in camera and ex parte the application, order, and such other materials relating to the physical search at issue needed to determine whether the physical search of the aggrieved person was lawfully authorized and conducted. If the court finds it necessary to make an accurate determination of the legality of the search, the court may disclose portions of the application, order, or other pertinent materials to the aggrieved person under appropriate security

[55] 50 U.S.C. § 1825(d). "Aggrieved person," as defined in 50 U.S.C. § 1821(2), "means a person whose premises, property, information, or material is the target of a physical search or any other person whose premises, property, information, or material was subject to physical search."

[56] 50 U.S.C. § 1825(e).

[57] 50 U.S.C. § 1825(f).

procedures and protective orders, or may require the Attorney General to provide a summary of such materials to the aggrieved person.[58]

If the U.S. district court makes a determination that the physical search was not lawfully authorized or conducted, then it must "suppress the evidence which was unlawfully obtained or derived from the physical search of the aggrieved person or otherwise grant the motion of the aggrieved person." If, on the other hand, the court finds that the physical search was lawfully authorized or conducted, the motion of the aggrieved person will be denied except to the extent that due process requires discovery or disclosure.[59]

If the U.S. district court grants a motion to suppress under 50 U.S.C. § 1825(h); deems a FISA physical search unlawfully authorized or conducted; or orders review or grants disclosure of applications, orders or other materials pertinent to a FISA physical search, that court order is final and binding on all federal and state courts except a U.S. Court of Appeals or the U.S. Supreme Court.[60]

As a general matter, where an emergency physical search is authorized under 50 U.S.C. § 1824(d), and a subsequent order approving the resulting search is not obtained, any U.S. person named in the application and any other U.S. persons subject to the search that the FISC judge deems appropriate in the interests of justice must be served with notice of the fact of the application and the period of the search, and must be advised as to whether information was or was not obtained during that period.[61] However, such notice may be postponed or suspended for a period not to exceed 90 days upon an ex parte showing of good cause to the judge, and, upon further good cause shown, the court must forego such notice altogether.[62]

Section 504(b) of P.L. 107-56, added a new 50 U.S.C. § 1825(k) to the statute, which deals with consultation by federal officers doing FISA searches with federal law enforcement officers. Under this new language, federal officers "who conduct physical searches to acquire foreign intelligence information" under 50 U.S.C. § 1821 *et seq.*, may consult with federal law enforcement officers:

> … to coordinate efforts to investigate or protect against
> (A) actual or potential attack or other grave hostile acts of a foreign power or an agent of a foreign power;

[58] 50 U.S.C. § 1825(g).
[59] 50 U.S.C. § 1825(h).
[60] 50 U.S.C. § 1825(i).
[61] 50 U.S.C. § 1825(j)(1).
[62] 50 U.S.C. § 1825(j)(2).

(B) sabotage or international terrorism by a foreign power or an agent of a foreign power; or
(C) clandestine intelligence activities by an intelligence service or network of a foreign power or by an agent of a foreign power.[63]

Such a coordination does not preclude certification required under 50 U.S.C. § 1823(a)(7) or entry of an order under 50 U.S.C. § 1824.[64]

50 U.S.C. § 1826 provides for semiannual congressional oversight of physical searches under FISA. The Attorney General is directed to "fully inform" the permanent Select Committee on Intelligence of the House of Representatives and the Select Committee on Intelligence of the Senate with respect to all physical searches conducted under 50 U.S.C. § 1821 *et seq.* Also on a semiannual basis, the Attorney General is required to provide a report to those committees and to the House and Senate Judiciary Committees setting forth: the total number of applications for orders approving FISA physical searches during the preceding 6 month period; the total number of those orders granted, modified, or denied; the number of such physical searches involving the residences, offices, or personal property of United States persons; and the number of occasions, if any, the Attorney General gave notice under 50 U.S.C. § 1825(b).[65]

Section 1827 imposes criminal sanctions for intentionally executing a physical search for foreign intelligence gathering purposes under color of law within the United States except as authorized by statute. In addition, criminal penalties attach to a conviction for intentionally disclosing or using information obtained by a physical search under color of law within the United States for the purpose of gathering intelligence information, where the offender knows or has reason to know that the information was obtained by a physical search not authorized by statute. In either case, this section provides that a person convicted of such an offense faces a fine of not more than $10,000,[66] imprisonment for not more than 5 years or both. Federal jurisdiction attaches where the offense is committed by an officer or employee of the United States, It is a defense to such a prosecution if the defendant was a law enforcement or investigative officer engaged in official duties and the physical search was authorized and conducted pursuant to a search warrant or court order by a court of competent jurisdiction.

---

[63] 50 U.S.C. § 1825(k)(1).
[64] 50 U.S.C. § 1825(k)(2).
[65] *See* fn. 64, *supra*, and accompanying text.
[66] this section was added in 1994 as Title III, Section 307 of P.L. 95-511, by P.L. 103-359, Title VIII, § 807(a)(3), 108 Stat. 3452. If a fine were to be imposed under the general fine provisions 18 U.S.C. § 3571, rather than under the offense provision, the maximum fine would be $250,000 for an individual.

In addition, an aggrieved person other than a foreign power or an agent of a foreign power as defined under section 1801(a) or 1801(b)(1)(A),[67] whose premises, property, information, or material within the United States was physically searched under FISA; or about whom information obtained by such a search was disclosed or used in violation of 50 U.S.C. § 1827, may bring a civil action for actual damages, punitive damages, and reasonable attorney's fees and other investigative and litigation costs reasonably incurred.[68]

In times of war, the President, through the Attorney General, may authorize physical searches under FISA without a court order to obtain foreign intelligence information for up to 15 days following a declaration of war by Congress.[69]

Pen Registers or Trap and Trace Devices[70] Used for Foreign Intelligence Gathering Purposes

Title IV of FISA, 50 U.S.C. § 1841 *et seq.*, was added in 1998, significantly amended by P.L. 107-56,[71] and amended further by Section 314(5) of P.L. 107-108. Under 50 U.S.C. § 1842(a)(1), notwithstanding any other provision of law, the Attorney General or a designated attorney for the Government may apply for an order or extension of an order authorizing or

[67] For definitions, *see* fn. 14, *supra*.

[68] 50 U.S.C. § 1828. Actual damages are defined to be "not less than liquidated damages of $1,000 or $100 per day for each violation, whichever is greater." 50 U.S.C. § 1828(1).

[69] 50 U.S.C. § 1829.

[70] Under 50 U.S.C. § 1841(2), the terms "pen register" and "trap and trace device" are given the meanings in 18 U.S.C. § 3127. Under Section 3127 "pen register"

> … means a device which records or decodes electronic or other impulses which identify the numbers dialed or otherwise transmitted on the telephone line to which such device is attached, but such term does not include any device used by a provider or customer of a wire or electronic communication service for billing, or recording as an incident to billing, for communications services provided by such provider or any device used by a provider or customer of a wire communication service for cost accounting or other like purposes in the ordinary course of its business;
> ….

As defined by 18 U.S.C. § 3127(4), "trap and trace device" "means a device which captures the incoming electronic or other impulses which identify the originating number of an instrument or device from which a wire or electronic communication was transmitted." 50 U.S.C. § 1841 is the section that defines terms applicable to the pen register and trap and trace device portions of FISA.

[71] Title IV of IFSA was added by Title VI, Sec. 601(2) of P.L. 105-272, on October 20, 1998, 112 Stat. 2405-2410., and amended by P.L. 107-56 and by P.L. 107-108.

approving the installation and use of a pen register or trap and trace device "*for any investigation to protect against international terrorism or clandestine intelligence activities, provided such investigation of a United States person is not conducted solely upon the basis of activities protected by the first amendment to the Constitution*" conducted by the Federal Bureau of Investigation (FBI) under guidelines approved by the Attorney General pursuant to E.O. 12333 or a successor order.[72] This authority is separate from the authority to conduct electronic surveillance under 50 U.S.C. § 1801 *et seq.*[73]

Each such application is made in writing upon oath or affirmation to a FISC judge or to a U.S. magistrate judge publicly designated by the Chief Justice of the United States to hear such applications and grant orders approving installation of pen registers or trap and trace devices on behalf of a FISC judge. The application must be approved by the Attorney General or a designated attorney for the Government. Each application must identify the federal officer seeking to use the pen register or trap and trace device sought in the application. It must also include a certification by the applicant "*that the information likely to be obtained is relevant to an ongoing investigation to protect against international terrorism or clandestine intelligence activities, provided that such investigation of a United States person is not conducted solely upon the basis of activities protected by the first amendment to the Constitution.*"[74]

---

[72] The italicized language was added by P.L. 107-56, Section 214(a)(1), replacing language which had read "for any investigation to gather foreign intelligence information or information concerning international terrorism."

[73] 50 U.S.C. § 1842(a)(2).

[74] This language, added by P.L. 107-56, Section 214(a)(2), replaced stricken language which read:

> (2) a certification by the applicant that the information to be obtained is relevant to an ongoing foreign intelligence or international terrorism investigation being conducted by the Federal Bureau of Investigation under guidelines approved by the Attorney General; and
>
> (3) information which demonstrates that there is reason to believe that the telephone line to which the pen register or trap and trace device is to be attached, or the communication instrument or device to be covered by the pen register or trap and trace device, has been or is about to be used in communication with –
>
> > (A) an individual who is engaging or has engaged in international terrorism or clandestine intelligence activities that involve or may involve a violation of the criminal laws of the United States; or
> >
> > (B) a foreign power or agent of a foreign power under circumstances giving reason to believe that the communication concerns or concerned international terrorism or clandestine

Under 50 U.S.C. § 1842, as amended by P.L. 107-56, pen registers and trap and trace devices may now be installed and used not only to track telephone calls, but also other forms of electronic communication such as e-mail. Once an application is made under Section 1842, the judge[75] must enter an ex parte order[76] as requested or as modified approving the installation and

> intelligence activities that involve or may involve a violation of the criminal laws of the United States.

[75] This section refers simply to "judge." In light of 50 U.S.C. § 1842(b), it would appear that this may refer to either a FISC judge or a U.S. magistrate judge designated by the Chief Justice under Section 1842(b)(2) to hear applications for and grant orders approving installation and use of pen registers or trap and trace devices on behalf of a FISC judge. The legislative history on this provision does not appear to clarify this point. The language was included in the bill reported out as an original measure by the Senate Select Committee on Intelligence, S. 2052, as Sec. 601. The Committee's report, S. Rept. 105-185, indicates that magistrate judges were included in the legislation to parallel their use in connection with receipt of applications and approval of pen registers and trap and trace devices in the context of criminal investigations, but reflected the Committee's understanding that the authority provided in the legislation to designate magistrate judges to consider applications for pen registers and trap and trace devices in the foreign intelligence gathering context would be closely monitored by the Department of Justice and this designation authority would not be exercised until the Committee was briefed on the compelling need for such designations, as reflected, for example, through statistical information on the frequency of applications to the FISC under the new procedure. S. Rept. 105-185, at 28 (May 7, 1998). The provision creating on pen registers and trap and trace devices in foreign intelligence and international terrorism investigations, Sec. 601 of the bill as passed, was among those included in the conference version of H.R. 3694 which was passed in lieu of S. 2052. H. Conference Rept. 105-80, at 32 (October 5, 1998).

[76] Under 50 U.S.C. § 1842(d)(2)(A), such an order

(A) shall specify –

> *(i) the identity, if known, of the person who is the subject of the investigation;*
> *(ii) the identity, if known, of the person to whom is leased or in whose name is listed the telephone line or other facility to which the pen register or trap and trace device is to be attached or applied;*
> *(iii) the attributes of the communications to which the order applies, such as the number or other identifies, and, if known, the location of the telephone line or other facility to which the pen register or trap and trace device is to be attached or applied and, in the case of a trap and trace device, the geographic limits of the trap and trace order.*

(B) shall direct that –

> (i) upon request of the applicant, the provider of a wire or electronic communication service, landlord, custodian, or other person shall furnish any information, facilities, or technical assistance necessary to accomplish the installation and operation of the pen register or trap and trace device in such a manner as will protect its secrecy and produce a minimum amount of interference with the services that such provider, landlord, custodian, or other person is providing the person concerned;

use of a pen register or trap and trace device if the application meets the requirements of that section.

Section 1843 of Title 18 of the United States Code focuses upon authorization for installation and use of a pen register or trap and trace device under FISA during specified types of emergencies. This provision applies when the Attorney General makes a reasonable determination that:

> (1) an emergency requires the installation and use of a pen register or trap and trace device to obtain foreign intelligence information not concerning a United States person or information to protect against international terrorism or clandestine intelligence activities, provided that such investigation of a United States person is not conducted solely upon the basis of activities protected by the first amendment to the Constitution before an order authorizing the installation and use of the pen register or trap and trace device, as the case may be, can with due diligence be obtained under section 1842 of this title; and (2) the factual basis for issuance of an order under section 1842(c) of this title to approve the

---

(ii) such provider, landlord, custodian, or other person –

(I) shall not disclose the existence of the investigation or of the pen register or trap and trace device to any person unless or until ordered by the court; and

(II) shall maintain, under security procedures approved by the Attorney General and the Director of Central Intelligence pursuant to section 1805(b)(2)(C) of this title, any records concerning the pen register or trap and trace device or the aid furnished; and

(iii) the applicant shall compensate such provider, landlord, custodian, or other person for reasonable expenses incurred by such provider, landlord, custodian, or other person in providing such information, facilities, or technical assistance.

The italicized portions of this section reflect amended language from P.L. 107-56, Section 214(a)(4).

P.L. 107-108, Section 314(a)(5)(B), replaced "of a court" at the end of 50 U.S.C. § 1842(f) with "of an order issued," so that the language now reads:

(f) No cause of action shall lie in any court against any provider of a wire or electronic communication service, landlord, custodian, or other person (including any officer, employee, agent, or other specified person thereof) that furnishes any information, facilities, or technical assistance under subsection (d) in accordance with the terms *of an order issued* under this section.

(Emphasis added.) *Cf.*, 50 U.S.C. § 1805(f), which contains an immunity grant which, at first blush would appear to apply only to electronic surveillance under FISA, but which has been interpreted in H. Rept. 107-328, page 25, the conference committee accompanying H.R. 2883, which became P.L. 107-108, to apply to electronic surveillance, physical searches and pen register and trap and trace devices. See discussion at fn. 32, *supra*.

> installation and use of the pen register or trap and trace device, as the case may be, exists.[77]

Upon making such a determination, the Attorney General may authorize the installation and use of a pen register or trap and trace device for this purpose if two criteria are met. First, the Attorney General or his designee must inform a judge referred to in Section 1842(b)[78] at the time of the emergency authorization that the decision to install and use the pen register or trap and trace device has been made. Second, an application for a court order authorizing a pen register or trap and trace device under 50 U.S.C. § 1842(a)(1) must be made to the judge as soon as practicable, but no later than 48 hours after the emergency authorization.[79] If no order approving the installation and use of a pen register or trap and trace device is forthcoming, then the installation and use of such pen register or trap and trace device must terminate at the earlier of the time when the information sought is obtained, the time when the application for the order is denied under 50 U.S.C. § 1842, or the expiration of 48 hours from the time the Attorney General made his emergency authorization.[80]

If an application for an order sought under Section 1843(a)(2) is denied, or if the installation and use of the pen register or trap and trace device is terminated, and no order approving it is issued under 50 U.S.C. § 1842(b)(2), then no information obtained or evidence derived from the use of the pen register or trap and trace device may be received in evidence or disclosed in any trial, hearing or other proceeding in any court, grand jury, department, office, agency, regulatory body, legislative committee or other federal state or local authority. Furthermore, in such circumstances, no information concerning a United States person acquired from the use of the pen register or trap and trace device may later be used or disclosed in any other way by federal officers or employees without consent of the U.S. person involved, with one exception. If the Attorney General approves the disclosure because the information indicates a threat of death or serious bodily harm to anyone, then disclosure without consent of the U.S. person involved is permitted.[81]

---

[77] 50 U.S.C. § 1843(b) (italics reflect language added by P.L. 107-56, § 214(b), in place of language which read "foreign intelligence information or information concerning international terrorism.") Similar language was inserted in 50 U.S.C. § 1843(a) by P.L. 107-56, § 214(b)(1), in place of language that paralleled that stricken from subsection 1843(b).

[78] See discussion of the term "judge" as used in Section 1842(b) in fn. 86, *supra*.

[79] 50 U.S.C. § 1843(a).

[80] 50 U.S.C. § 1843(c)(1).

[81] 50 U.S.C. § 1843(c)(2).

If Congress declares war, then, notwithstanding any other provision of law, the President, through the Attorney General, may authorize use of a pen register or trap and trace device without a court order to acquire foreign intelligence information for up to 15 calendar days after the declaration of war.[82]

50 U.S.C. § 1845 sets parameter with respect to the use of information obtained through the use of a pen register or trap and trace device under 50 U.S.C. § 1841 *et seq*. Federal officers and employees may only use or disclose such information with respect to a U.S. person without the consent of that person in accordance with Section 1845.[83] Any disclosure by a Federal officer or employee of information acquired pursuant to FISA from a pen register or trap and trace device must be for a lawful purpose.[84] Disclosure for law enforcement purposes of information acquired under 50 U.S.C. § 1841 *et seq*. is only permitted where the disclosure is accompanied by a statement that the information and any derivative information may only be used in a criminal proceeding with the advance authorization of the Attorney General.[85]

Under 50 U.S.C. § 1845(c), when the United States intends to enter into evidence, use, or disclose information obtained by or derived from a FISA pen register or trap and trace device against an aggrieved person[86] in any federal trial, hearing, or proceeding, notice requirements must be satisfied. The Government, before the trial, hearing, or proceeding or a reasonable time before the information is to be proffered, used or disclosed, must give notice of its intent both to the aggrieved person involved[87] and to the court or other authority in which the information is to be disclosed or used.

If a state or local government intends to enter into evidence, use, or disclose information obtained or derived from such a trap and trace device

---

[82] 50 U.S.C. § 1844.

[83] 50 U.S.C. § 1845(a)(1).

[84] 50 U.S.C. § 1845(a)(2).

[85] 50 U.S.C. § 1845(b).

[86] "Aggrieved person" is defined in 50 U.S.C. § 1841(3) for purposes of 50 U.S.C. § 1841 *et seq*. as any person:
(A) whose telephone line was subject to the installation or use of a pen register or trap and trace device authorized by subchapter IV [50 U.S.C. § 1841 et seq.]; or
(B) whose communication instrument or device was subject to the use of a pen register or trap and trace device authorized by subchapter IV to capture incoming electronic or other communications impulses.

[87] The statute refers to notice to the "aggrieved person." Here it is using this term in the context of a pen register or trap and trace device, as defined in 50 U.S.C. § 1841(3) (see fn. 98, *supra*). This term is also defined in both 50 U.S.C. § 1801(k) (in the context of electronic surveillance, see fn. 35, *supra*) and 1825(d) (in the context of a physical search, see fn. 66, *supra*).

against an aggrieved person in a state or local trial, hearing or proceeding, it must give notice to the aggrieved person and to the Attorney General of the United States of the state or local government's intent to disclose or use the information.[88]

The aggrieved person in either case may move to suppress the evidence obtained or derived from a FISA pen register or trap and trace device on one of two grounds: that the information was unlawfully acquired; or that the use of the pen register or trap and trace device was not made in conformity with an order of authorization or approval under 50 U.S.C. § 1841 *et seq.*[89]

If notice is given under 50 U.S.C. § 1845(c) or (d), or a motion or request is made to suppress or to discover or obtain any applications, orders, or other materials relating to use of a FISA pen register or trap and trace device or information obtained by or derived from such use, the Attorney General may have national security concerns with respect to the effect of such disclosure or of an adversary hearing. If he files an affidavit under oath that disclosure or any adversary hearing would harm the national security of the United States, the United States district court in which the motion or request is made, or where the motion or request is made before another authority, the U.S. district court in the same district, shall review *in camera* and *ex parte* the application, order, and other relevant materials to determine whether the use of the pen register or trap and trace device was lawfully authorized and conducted.[90] In do doing, the court may only disclose portions of the application, order or materials to the aggrieved person or order the Attorney General to provide the aggrieved person with a summary of these materials if that disclosure is necessary to making an accurate determination of the legality of the use of the pen register or trap and trace device.[91]

Should the court find that the pen register or trap and trace device was not lawfully authorized or conducted, it may suppress the unlawfully obtained or derived evidence or "otherwise grant the motion of the aggrieved person."[92] On the other hand, if the court finds the pen register or trap and trace device lawfully authorized and conducted, it may deny the aggrieved person's motion except to the extent discovery or disclosure is required by due process.[93] Any U.S. district court orders granting motions or request under Section 1845(g), finding unlawfully authorized or conducted the use

[88] 50 U.S.C. § 1845(d).
[89] 50 U.S.C. § 1845(e).
[90] 50 U.S.C. § 1845(f)(1).
[91] 50 U.S.C. § 1845(f)(2).
[92] 50 U.S.C. § 1845(g)(1).
[93] 50 U.S.C. § 1845(g)(2).

of a pen register or trap and trace device, or requiring review or granting disclosure of applications, orders or other materials regarding installation and use of a pen register or trap and trace device are deemed final orders. They are binding on all federal and state courts except U.S. courts of appeals and the U.S. Supreme Court.[94]

Section 1846 deal with congressional oversight of the use of FISA pen registers and trap and trace devices. It requires the Attorney General semiannually to fully inform the House Permanent Select Committee on Intelligence and the Senate Select Committee on Intelligence regarding all FISA uses of pen registers and trap and trace devices. In addition, the Attorney General, on a semi-annual basis, must report to the House Permanent Select Committee on Intelligence, the Senate Select Committee on Intelligence, the House Judiciary Committee and the Senate Judiciary Committee on the total number of applications made for orders approving the use of such pen registers and trap and trace devices and the total number of such orders granted, modified, or denied during the previous 6 month period.

Access to Certain Business Records for Foreign Intelligence Purposes

Also added in 1998, Title V of FISA, 50 U.S.C. § 1861 *et seq.*, was substantially changed by P.L. 107-56 and modified further by P.L. 107-108.[95] Although denominated "access to certain business records for foreign

---

[94] 50 U.S.C. § 1845(h).

[95] Title V of FISA was added by Title VI, Sec. 602, of P.L. 105-272, on October 20, 1998, 112 Stat. 2411-12, and significantly amended by P.L. 107-56 and P.L. 107-108. The prior version of 50 U.S.C. § 1861 provided definitions for "foreign power," "agent of a foreign power," "Foreign intelligence information," "international terrorism," and "Attorney General," "common carrier," "physical storage facility," "public accommodation facility," and "vehicle rental facility" for purposes of 50 U.S.C. § 1861 *et seq.* The prior version of Section 1862 was much more narrowly drawn than the new version added in P.L. 107-56 and amended by P.L. 107-108. The earlier version read:

> (a) The Director of the Federal Bureau of Investigation or a designee of the Director (whose rank shall be no lower than Assistant Special Agent in Charge) may make an application for an order authorizing a common carrier, public accommodation facility, physical storage facility, or vehicle rental facility to release records in its possession for an investigation to gather foreign intelligence information or an investigation concerning international terrorism which investigation is being conducted by the Federal Bureau of Investigation under such guidelines as the Attorney General approves pursuant to Executive Order No. 12333, or a successor order.

intelligence and international terrorism investigations" the reach of Section 1861, as amended by the USA PATRIOT Act and P.L. 107-108, is now

---

(b) Each application under this section –

(1) shall be made to –

(A) a judge of the court established by section 1803(a) of this title; or

(B) a United States Magistrate Judge under chapter 43 of Title 28 [28 U.S.C. § 631 *et seq.*], who is publicly designated by the Chief Justice of the United States to have the power to her applications and grant orders for the release of records under this section on behalf of a judge of that court; and

(2) shall specify that –

(A) the records concerned are sought for an investigation described in subsection (a); and

(B) there are specific and articulable facts giving reason to believe that the person to whom the records pertain is a foreign power or an agent of a foreign power.

(c)(1) Upon application made pursuant to this section, the judge shall enter an ex parte order as requested, or as modified, approving the release of records if the judge find that the application satisfied the requirements of this section.

(2) An order under this subsection shall not disclose that it is issued for purposes of an investigation described in subsection (a).

(d)(1) Any common carrier, public accommodation facility, physical storage facility, or vehicle rental facility shall comply with an order under subsection (c).

(2) No common carrier, public accommodation facility, physical storage facility, or vehicle rental facility, or officer, employee, or agent thereof, shall disclose to any person (other than those officers, agents, or employees of such common carrier, public accommodation facility, physical storage facility, or vehicle rental facility necessary to fulfill the requirement to disclose information to the Federal Bureau of Investigation under this section) that the Federal Bureau of Investigation has sought or obtained records pursuant to an order under this section.

Congressional oversight was covered under the prior provisions by 50 U.S.C. § 1863, which was similar, but not identical to the new Section 1862. The former Section 1863 stated:

(a) On a semiannual basis, the Attorney General shall fully inform the Permanent Select Committee on Intelligence of the House of Representatives and the Select Committee on Intelligence of the Senate concerning all request for records under this subchapter 50 U.S.C. § 1861 *et seq.*].

(b) On a semiannual basis, the Attorney General shall provide to the Committees on the Judiciary of the House of Representatives and the Senate a report setting forth with respect to the preceding 6-month period –

(1) the total number of applications made for orders approving requests for records under this subchapter [50 U.S.C. § 1861 *et seq.*,]; and

(2) the total number of such orders either granted, modified, or denied.

substantially broader than business records alone. Under 50 U.S.C. § 1861(a)(1), the Director of the FBI, or his designee (who must be at the Assistant Special Agent in Charge level or higher in rank) may apply for an order requiring

> ... the production of any tangible things (including books, records, papers, documents, and other items) for an investigation *to obtain foreign intelligence information not concerning a United States person or* to protect against international terrorism or clandestine intelligence activities, provided that such investigation of a United States person is not conducted solely upon the basis of activities protected by the first amendment to the Constitution.[96]

Subsection 1861(a)(2) requires that such an investigation must be conducted under guidelines approved by the Attorney General under E.O. 12333 or a successor order and prohibits such an investigation of a United States person based solely upon First Amendment protected activities.

An application for an order under Section 1861 must be made to an FISC judge or to a U.S. magistrate judge publicly designated by the Chief Justice of the United States to hear such applications and grant such orders for the production of tangible things on behalf of an FISC judge.[97] The

---

[96] The italicized portion of Section 1861(a)(1) was added by Section 314(a)(6) of P.L. 107-108. H. Rept. 107-328, the conference report to accompany H.R. 2883, the Intelligence Authorization Act for Fiscal Year 2002 (which became P.L. 107-108), at page 24, describes the purpose of this addition as follows:

> Section 215 of the USA PATRIOT Act of 2001 amended title V of the FISA, adding a new section 501 [50 U.S.C. § 1861]. Section 501(a) now authorizes the director of the FBI to apply for a court order to produce certain records "For an investigation to protect against international terrorism or clandestine intelligence activities." Section 501(b)(2) directs that the application for such records specify that the purpose of the investigation is to "obtain foreign intelligence information not concerning a United States person." However, section 501(a)(1), which generally authorizes the applications, does not contain equivalent language. Thus, subsections (a)(1) and (b)(2) now appear inconsistent.
>
> The conferees agreed to a provision which adds the phrase "to obtain foreign intelligence information not concerning a United States person or" to section 501(a)(1). This would make the language of section 501(a)(1) consistent with the legislative history of section 215 of the USA PATRIOT Act (*see* 147 Cong. Res. S11006 (daily ed. Oct. 25, 2002)(sectional analysis)) and with the language of section 214 of the USA PATRIOT Act (authorizing an application for an order to use pen registers and trap and trace devices to "obtain foreign intelligence information not concerning a United States person.").

[97] 50 U.S.C. § 1861(b)(1).

application must specify that the "records"[98] are sought for "an authorized investigation conducted in accordance with [50 U.S.C. § 1862(a)(2)] to obtain foreign intelligence information not concerning a United States person or to protect against international terrorism or clandestine intelligence activities."[99] When such an application is made, the judge must enter an *ex parte* order "as requested, or as modified, approving the release of records if the judge finds that the application meets the requirements of this section."[100] Such an order shall not disclose that it is issued for purposes of an investigation under 50 U.S.C. § 1861(a).[101] Subsection 1861(d) prohibits any person to disclose that the FBI has sought or obtained tangible things under Section 1861, except where the disclosure is made to persons necessary to the production of tangible things involved. Subsection 1861(e) precludes liability for persons who, in good faith, produce tangible things under such a Section 1861 order. It further indicates that production does not constitute a waiver of any privilege in any other proceeding or context.

50 U.S.C. § 1862 deals with congressional oversight. Subsection 1862(a) requires the Attorney General semiannually to fully inform the House Permanent Select Committee on Intelligence and the Senate Select Committee on Intelligence regarding all request for production of tangible things under Section 1861.[102] Subsection 1962(b) requires the Attorney General to report to the House and Senate Judiciary Committees on the total number of applications for Section 1861 orders for production of tangible things and on the total number of such orders granted, modified, or denied during the previous 6 months.

---

[98] While the language refers to "records," it is worthy of note that the authority conferred upon the Director of the FBI or his designee under Section 1861(a) encompasses applications for orders requiring production of "any tangible thing (including books, records, papers, documents, and other items)." One might argue, therefore, that for Subsection 1861(a)(1) and Subsection 1861(b)(2) to be read in harmony, a court might interpret "records" more broadly to cover "any tangible thing." On the other hand, if, by virtue of the specific reference in Subsection 1861(a)(1) to "records" as only one of many types of "tangible things," the term "records" in Subsection 1861(b)(2) were to be read narrowly, it might lead to some confusion as to the nature and scope of any specification that might be required where an application seeking production of types of tangible things other than records is involved.

[99] 50 U.S.C. § 1861(b)(2).

[100] 50 U.S.C. § 1861(c)(1).

[101] 50 U.S.C. § 1861(c)(2).

[102] Section 314(a)(7) of P.L. 107-108 corrected two references in 50 U.S.C. § 1862 as passed in the USA PATRIOT Act. P.L. 107-108 replaced "section 1842 of this title" with "section 1861 of this title," in both places in 50 U.S.C. § 1862 where it appeared.

NEW PRIVATE RIGHT OF ACTION

In addition to provisions which amended FISA explicitly, other provisions of the USA PATRIOT Act touched upon FISA, at least tangentially. For example, Section 223 of the Act, among other things, created a new 18 U.S.C. § 2712. This new section, in part, created an exclusive private right of action for any person aggrieved by any willful violation of sections 106(a), 305(a), or 405(a) of FISA (50 U.S.C. §§ 1806(a), 1825(a), 1845(a), respectively) to be brought against the Untied States in U.S. district court to recover money damages. Such monetary relief would amount to either actual damages or $10,000, whichever is greater; and reasonably incurred litigation costs. It also set forth applicable procedures.[103]

USA PATRIOT ACT SUNSET PROVISION

Section 224 of the USA PATRIOT Act set a sunset for many of the provisions in the Act of December 31, 2005. Among those provisions which will sunset pursuant to this are all of the amendments to FISA, and subsequent amendments thereto, except the provision which increased the number of FISC judges from 7 to 11 (Section 208 of P.L. 107-56). Section 25 also excepts from the application of the sunset provision any particular foreign intelligence investigations that began before December 31, 2005, or any particular offenses or potential offenses which began or occurred before December 31, 2005. As to those particular investigations or offenses, applicable provisions would continue in effect.

[103] Another provision, Section 901 of the USA PATRIOT Act, amended 50 U.S.C. § 403-3(c) (Section 103(c) of the National Security Act of 1947) regarding the responsibilities of the Director of Central Intelligence (DCI). The amendment added to those authorities and responsibilities, placing upon the DCI the responsibility for the establishment of

> ... requirements and priorities for foreign intelligence information to be collected under the Foreign Intelligence Surveillance Act of 1978 (50 U.S.C. § 1801 et seq.), and provide assistance to the Attorney General to ensure that information derived from electronic surveillance or physical searches under that Act is disseminated so it may be used efficiently and effectively for foreign intelligence purposes, except that the Director shall have no authority to direct, manage, or undertake electronic surveillance or physical search operations pursuant to that Act unless otherwise authorized by statute or Executive order.

Chapter 4

CONCLUSION

The Foreign Intelligence Surveillance Act, as amended, provides a statutory structure to be followed where electronic surveillance, 50 U.S.C. § 1801 *et seq*., physical searches, 50 U.S.C. § 1821 *et seq*., or pen registers or trap and trace devices, 50 U.S.C. § 1841 *et seq*., for foreign intelligence gathering purposes are contemplated. It creates enhanced procedural protections where a United States person is involved, while setting somewhat less stringent standards where the surveillance involves foreign powers or agents of foreign powers. With its detailed statutory structure, it appears intended to protect personal liberties safeguarded by the First and Fourth Amendments while providing a means to ensure national security interests.

The USA PATRIOT Act, P.L. 107-56, increased the number of FISC judges from 7 to 11, while expanding the availability of FISA electronic surveillance, physical searches and pen registers and trap and trace devices. For example, under P.L. 107-56, an application for a court order permitting electronic surveillance or a physical search under FISA is now permissible where "a significant" purpose of the surveillance or physical search, rather than "the" purpose or, as interpreted by some courts, the primary purpose of the surveillance is to gather foreign intelligence information. While the previous language withstood constitutional challenge, the constitutional sufficiency of the change in the FISA procedures under the Fourth Amendment is, as yet, untested.

The USA PATRIOT Act also amended FISA to allow court orders permitting so-called multipoint or "roving" electronic surveillance, where the orders to not require particularity with respect to the identification of the instrument, place, or facility to be intercepted, upon a finding by the court that the actions of the target of the surveillance are likely to thwart such identification. P.L. 107-108 further clarified this authority.

Under the Act, pen registers and trap and trace devices may now be authorized for e-mails as well as telephone conversations. In addition, the Act expanded the previous FBI access to business records, permitting court ordered access in connection with a foreign intelligence or international terrorism investigation not just to business records held by common carriers, public accommodation facilities, physical storage facilities, and vehicle rental facilities, but to any tangible things.

While expanding the authorities available for foreign intelligence investigations, FISA, as amended by the USA PATRIOT Act and the Intelligence Authorization Act for FY2002, also contains broader protections for those who may be the target of the various investigative techniques involved. For example, whether the circumstances involve electronic surveillance, physical searches, pen registers, or trap and trace devices of access to business records and other tangible items, FISA, as amended by the USA PATRIOT Act, does not permit the court to grant orders based solely upon a United States person's exercise of First Amendment rights.[1]

In addition, P.L. 107-56 created a new private right of action for persons aggrieved by inappropriate disclosure or use of information gleaned or derived from electronic surveillance, physical searches or the use of pen registers or trap and trace devices. These claims can be brought against the United States for certain willful violations by government personnel.

Finally, the inclusion of a sunset provision for the FISA changes made in the USA PATRIOT Act, with the exception of the increase in the number of FISC judges, provides an opportunity for the new authorities to be utilized and considered, and an opportunity for the Congress to revisit them in light of that experience.

---

[1] *See, e.g.*, U.S.C. §§ 1805(a)(3)(A), 1824(a)(3)(A), 1842(a)(1), 1843(b), 1861(a)(1), and 1861(a)(2).

INDEX

A

B

C

D

E

F

G

H

I

J

L

M

N

O

P